About *10 Guideline Principles*

In martial arts, learning techniques without understanding the principles that support the forms and use of various techniques in different situations can be ineffectual and even counterproductive. Likewise, living moment-to-moment without having a set of principles that support our behavior in every context is a recipe for misunderstanding and chaos. The world is chaotic enough without each of us adding to the chaos. In this book, *10 Guideline Principles*, Tony Annesi provides us with a set of principles that can guide our behavior, helping us to remain true to ourselves, no matter what is happening around us. I'm excited to recommend this book to anyone open to establishing excellent fundamental principles for their daily lives.   —Richard Raben, Ph.D.

Whose advice is worth hearing? Life coaches? Academics? Therapists? Poets? Philosophers? Clerics? Physicists? All of the above, depending? How about an internationally decorated martial artist and teacher, an entrepreneur, author of fiction and nonfiction, and observer of the cultural scene, rolled into one? Tony Annesi has written a short book distilling what he has learned from a range of experiences and achievements into ten flexible principles pointed enough to guide a life well.

He speaks persuasively for truthfulness, for courage, for reasonableness, for individuality, for change that begins inside. Through engaging advice, quotes, analysis, and personal anecdotes, Tony steers between radical individualism and communitarianism, traditionalism and noveltyism, and reason and emotion, to chart a path that is reasonable, flexible, and vigorous.   —C. Wesley DeMarco, Ph.D.

Sensei Tony is very likely the most intelligent, fascinating, and — more than anything else — honorable and high-character human being… that you've never heard of, and that's only because he built his reputation within a very select niche, Martial Arts. With that in mind, I'll simply suggest that in devouring the exquisite teachings contained in this book that you'll be learning from a combination of *The Karate Kid*'s Mr. Miyagi and the philosopher, Aristotle. May I suggest not only reading —and studying —it yourself, but making sure your children read it the very moment they are old enough to take responsibility for the thoughts, philosophies, and actions that will determine their happiness in life.

      — Bob Burg, coauthor of *The Go-Giver* and author of *Adversaries into Allies*

10 GUIDELINE PRINCIPLES

Finding One's Way in a Messy World

DISCLAIMER:

The author has no intention to slight, defame, or offend any person living or dead and apologizes for any factual errors that may unwittingly be presented in these pages.

10 Guideline Principles

Finding One's Way in a Messy World

CONTENTS

My Guideline Principles

"Nothing brings you peace like the triumph of principles."
—Ralph Waldo Emerson

TRUTH:

1. Neither tell nor believe lies about "the other side" just because you want them to be true;

2. Dare to be scrupulously honest even if it means losing—winning via a lie will gradually destroy you and your cause, as well;

3. Reframe the facts to make yourself feel better, if you like, but don't represent that reframe as the objective truth.

COURAGE:

4. Dare to lose in love, in business, and in life—losing never lasts, but if you win all the time, you are either cheating or playing with inferior opponents;

5. "What could have been" can be painful and debilitating—realize the simple fact that it could not have been.

INDEPENDENCE:

6. Support or contribute to any cause you can validate, not one that simply sounds good—an un-validated cause may represent the opposite of what you value. Refrain, however, from membership in movements, parties, or protests. Not only do their beliefs and means tend to change over time, but your joining may make you feel obligated to defend what they stand for, rather than think for yourself.

CONVENTIONS:

7. Conventions and customs are not unassailable, but without them there is chaos. Argue against them, if you wish, but in so doing, present an alternative that will work. If, over time, you find your alternative does not work, accept that the original convention, albeit flawed, has value. Neither NEW nor OLD is necessarily better. All things must prove their objective worth; otherwise, they are just personal preferences.

EMOTION vs. RATIONALITY:

8. If an emotional message is swaying your opinion, try to understand the core belief in the message behind the emotions. Even the most forceful assertion is not the same as evidence;

9. Emotions help us identify our values; they do not help us determine how to appraise them, obtain them, or keep them. Only rationality can do that.

BIAS:

10. Prejudgment and bias may be difficult to avoid completely since they are psychological shortcuts to evaluating someone or something. However, discriminating because of a bias is as irrational as assuming that individuals cannot think or act in any way, except the way their group thinks or acts. Both groupthink and the assumption of groupthink eliminate individualism. Individuals are, in the end, the smallest minority.

PREFACE:

Why Guideline Principles?

And What's this Messy World?

Originally, I came up with five guidelines that I found I was using to wend my way through an occasionally uncongenial Facebook community. Realizing that the five guidelines implied other relevant ideas, I extended the list to ten. These are principles that have worked for me, personally. They are generic in the sense that I have applied them not only to social media, but also to my life in general. They are not sent down from on high (except that my little brain tends to be higher than most of my body), however they are products of a lot of reflection. We are individuals, each with different mindset and different priorities, so you may feel these guidelines are not for you. I offer them for your trial and reflection because I can make a respectable case for following them. If you agree (or if you cannot find any counter-arguments), I would encourage you to try them to see if they compliment your mindset or if they challenge you to adjust that mindset.

You might think the title should be "10 Guiding Principles", rather than "10 Guideline Principles". I consciously chose "Guideline" instead of "Guiding" for a reason—one that is nuanced. For me, these principles suggest a condensed set of beliefs, values, or attitudes that one can use as a compass when one is unsure of the way to go. Because "guideline" is seldom used as an adjective, I hope that the reader's emphasis will be on the less rigid Guideline concept rather than on the more rigid idea of Principles. Of course, I take my principles seriously and do not want to follow them haphazardly. To do so would be falling into the "situation ethics" trap, a sort of "cafeteria consideration", i.e. being serious about principles unless some temptation convinces me to be less serious about them. I am sure someone somewhere will discover exceptions to these guidelines that I would support, but that would be a rare occurrence, and that would not sustain a case for "speaking out of both sides of my mouth".

Those who reject situation ethics in favor of absolute ethics often fall into a rigidity trap in which they refuse to see that two or more of their vaunted principles may have collided and that the situation may call for a clarification of, rather than inflexible obedience to, one of those principles. For this reason, I do not use the term "rule" or "law". I prefer the word Guideline (sounds kind of loose, doesn't it?) to modify the word Principles (sounds a bit more unbending, doesn't it?). When an advocate is too rigid, he/she may easily be caught staunchly standing up for a principle and then saying, "Except in the following situations," thus appearing inconsistent at best and hypocritical at worst.

These guideline principles are listed under six areas of thought: Truth, Courage, Independence, Conventions, Emotions vs. Rationality, and Bias. These areas intertwine, as you will begin to understand as you read. Of course, these are not the only intellectual/psychological areas in which there can be guideline principles. Similarly, the ten principles that make up the material of this book are not the only principles that have guided me, but they have become the most important, at least in recent years. That may be due to my personal experiences in life or because life has gotten messier or a mixture of both. But that is why they are my Guideline Principles.

Finally, in order to be a bit more inclusive without destroying the simplicity of a little book with only ten guidelines, there will be some corollaries and supplementary principles here and there, which I note in bold print.

To those readers of a more rigid character: I am not attempting to rewrite The Ten Commandments, The Code of Hammurabi, Solon's Reforms, or even Washington Carver's 8 Rules (see appendix).

To ultra-flexible readers that resist the idea that principles should arbitrate a decision, and prefer to use their intuition, I ask, "What do you think your intuition is based on, Punkie?" Consciously or unconsciously, we decide which way to go based on spontaneous self-interest (intuition) or long-term self-interest (intuition challenged and adjusted by reasoned principles). And this leads me to my first Supplementary Principle: Rational Self-interest is broad, long-term self-interest that includes the interests of other people whom we value or upon whom we depend. As such, rational self-interest is a virtue rather than a transgression or an immorality.

Our contemporary world is a messy one. Rather than living in a country (the USA) that was at one time a bastion of ideals to which much of the world aspired, we live in a world in which many people consider the USA just one of the players in a much larger panoply of nations. Communications and global enterprise have made the world not only smaller, but also more uncomfortably crowded in that smaller space. You are trapped in your cyber-neighborhood, no matter how wide it ranges, and that neighborhood has become congested. Friends and associates from other areas of your country and from other countries challenge your ideals on the premise that your ideals are no longer worthy of aspiration.

For most people in the USA, at least through the 1980s, if you didn't like your physical neighborhood, you could live without vexation within your personal domicile. If you didn't like your city, your state, or even your area of the country, you could move to someplace that made you feel more comfortable. Today, your friends, not only your immediate friends, but also your long lost friends about whom you have fond memories, are a few keystrokes away. They often espouse preferences and concepts that you would never have expected of them. Not only do your cyber-neighbors symbolically trample on your lawn, but they also claim that it isn't really your lawn! You now have to defend, even reestablish, your rights before you can attack their disregard for those rights.

One of the reasons people are more and more willing to join a group, a cause, a movement, or a party is that membership will make their new neighborhood manageable. Their lawns will be safe from being trampled and they know they will not feel pressed to defend themselves or respond to a friend's angry Tweet or Post. In fact, they will not have to even discuss any sensitive subject that could potentially damage a friendship. Instead, they will put their former friends (with whom they have disagreements) on hold until they want to contact them again on some mutually agreeable (and therefore comfortable) subject. They will spend the majority of their time within their group, with those they seem to agree with, taking their direction, their attitudes, and their lines of reasoning (to the extent that they care to have lines of reasoning) from those associates that seem to have the cleverest quips. Ironically, they will create divisions because of the technology that has brought us together.

Our easy access both to information and to others whom we know, or that we are coming to know, makes us vulnerable to both information overload and more frequent disputes. If we are not equipped to intellectually vie for victory in those disputes, we seek shelter with those who seem to be better equipped to contend. When we not only take a side, but also secure a niche, we are all snuggly and cared-for again, neither having to engage in the intellectual labor of figuring out our own points of view, nor having to deal with the clever, if often irrational, thrusts from those acquaintances that seem to be moving their mobile homes too close to ours.

If your world is a glut of confusion, seeking refuge in a group may bring temporary comfort, but will not solve the problem. What if your group seems to run out of convincing arguments? Will you then change groups or will you simply slur the other, albeit more convincing, side?

I suggest that if you honestly try to improve yourself, adhere to a few guidelines that are fair and beneficial to both you and the wider world, and act accordingly, as best you can, you might just find your way through the Fire Swamp and into the castle (or at least away from the madding crowd).

INTRODUCTION:

How I Came to Write a Book about Principles

Sitting in Mr. Jakes' eighth grade science class, in the right-most row, second seat from the front, I suddenly came to a revelation. It would be easier and more productive if, instead of memorizing facts, I tried to understand how things worked in general, that is, if I tried to understand concepts rather than concretes. Certainly the concretes (the individual facts) were important, but how they stacked together and formed an intellectual structure was at least as important. Henri Poincaré, the French mathematician and philosopher, said, "Science is built of facts, as a house is with stones. But a collection of facts is no more a science than a heap of stones is a house." Similarly, an intellectual structure is built upon facts organized by principles.

Poincaré also informs us that "To doubt everything and to believe everything are two equally convenient solutions; each save us from thinking." And, I submit, that is precisely where we find ourselves in the early part of the 21st century: either unwilling to put in the effort to think, or unable to think in a logical way, probably because we have been taught at a tender age that logic is variable according to the individual's point-of-view.

In junior high school, I bought a short novel called *Anthem* by Ayn Rand, about a future collectivist society. I bought it for two reasons: (1) because I had just read George

Orwell's *1984* and was planning to read Aldous Huxley's *Brave New World* and wanted a comparison, and (2) because *Anthem* would be a shorter read. (Note that reason #1 is a long-term self-interest while reason #2 is a short-term self-interest, as will be discussed below.) That novel led me to Rand's non-fiction, in which I especially noted those essays that emphasized, and gave examples of the value of concepts over concretes, an idea at which I had independently arrived.

When I was teaching Judo as a student at Brandeis University in the late 1960s, I taught almost exactly what I had been taught, afraid that I simply did not know enough to vary from the orthodox. Therefore, in my teaching, "concretes" dominated. By my second year of teaching, I occasionally innovated in the way I introduced techniques, and in creation of the exercises I used to get my information across to my fellow students; but unfortunately, I never considered the principles by which the techniques worked, except to understand the categories in which Dr. Jigoro Kano (the founder of Judo) had placed his required techniques. Categorization, if done reasonably, is a rudimentary recognition of principle, but if done too simplistically, can lead one astray and into biased judgment.

In the 1970s, having taken over a martial arts club that offered instruction in Judo, aiki-ju-jutsu, and karate, I began experimenting with referring to a short list of principles of physical action that I had created while I was teaching aiki-ju-jutsu techniques. Students loved this innovation because, armed with the list, they could analyze their own failed efforts rather than waiting for Sensei's (the teacher's) wisdom when I came around to correct them. Further, with my list of technical principles, my corrections made logical sense and therefore students did not have to robotically imitate what they were shown, rather they could adjust the movements to the partner with whom they were working. Thus, they modified the concretes (the technical specifics) to adhere to the principles in order to make the techniques work. They discovered that applying a principle to a learned concrete (a technique) was more valuable than performing a movement that looked perfect but had never been investigated via actual use.

A decade later, while preparing an article for the now defunct *Martial Arts World* magazine, I saw an article on aiki-ju-jutsu written and illustrated by Soke (system head) Don Angier. His aiki-ju-jutsu style was then called Shidare Yanagi Ryu (Weeping Willow Tradition) and was later changed to simply Yanagi Ryu. I started a correspondence with him and then a series of phone calls. To my knowledge, he was the only other person that taught martial arts via principles, and he had been doing so for more than a decade before I began to teach this way. Over the years, I learned an enormous amount from him about the aiki arts and about technical concepts and principles. That learning encouraged me to expand my study of principles to karate and then to martial arts in general. I summarized the most fundamental of these in a book called *The Principles of Advanced Budo*, in a DVD set by the same name, and decades later, expanded their number in series of Master Class seminars and DVDs.

I also wanted to know how martial arts improved peoples' lives beyond the obvious self-defense and exercise value. My intellectual inquiry led me to write a book on self-development through martial arts called *The Road to Mastery*. (These references can be found at www.bushido-kai.net.)

Self-development had been one of my interests for a very long time. Clearly, in high school, if I had wanted to improve my grades, I would have to study, which meant I would have to create a disciplined plan to follow. In doing so, I learned that I had to improve my means and methods in order to succeed at my end-goal. In essence, improving means and methods was an ancillary self-development (a short-term goal) to enhance the more overt self-development objective called scholastic knowledge (a long-term goal).

In an effort to continue my education after college, I had created self-study courses (French, Art History, and Philosophy being my favorites). These additional courses made me more knowledgeable about several subjects, thus rounding out my liberal arts degree, but they did not make me knowledgeable about how to apply that knowledge. Thinking that I understood French would do me no good unless I could read and converse in French. Knowing that late Gothic art came before late Renaissance art would do me no good unless I could tell a Giotto from a Raphael. Being able to discern Plato from Aristotle would be much more beneficial if I could see how their philosophies would influence later societies. In each case, I had to apply the knowledge that I had learned. The incentive to apply that knowledge was to better myself and, by extension, perhaps indirectly contribute to the betterment of the world around me. Supplementary Principle: **Knowledge is not know-how, and know-how is useless without purpose.** (NB: this supplementary principle will return when I discuss the values of rationality and emotion.)

I therefore read books and listened to cassette tapes by various self-development writers and lecturers such as Wayne Dyer and Tony Robbins, and a score of others. The best among them would not only instruct a new attitude to take, but would also lay down generic principles upon which that attitude depended.

Recently, I became interested in Professor Jordan Peterson's lectures on myth and meaning. That prompted me to read his *12 Rules for Life, An Antidote to Chaos*.

Even more recently, I walked into a local Barnes & Noble's to see a book called simply *Principles* by Ray Dalio. I knew Dalio was a successful investment authority, but since I did little with investments, I was more interested in the everyday principles he drew from his life, career, and business practices. At first, I was less impressed with Dalio's wisdom than with other sources that had influenced me; then, I realized that he was stating things I had already assimilated. (I guess he was wiser than I first thought.) I quote Dalio at the end of several of the main sections.

Okay, said I to me, I'm no business guru, nor professor of psychology, nor a famous lifestyle advisor, but I have a few "rules" by which I live (some of which never fail to surprise friends and associates) that have served me well. Hmm. Maybe this calls for my writing a book.

1.

TRUTH:

Neither tell nor believe lies about "the other side" just because you want them to be true.

Obviously, the simple way to say this is "Tell the truth," or, as Jordan Peterson writes in his *12 Rules for Life, An Antidote to Chaos*, "Tell the Truth, or At Least Don't Lie". As with several of my principles, I do not make the obvious, traditional, or simpler statement of a concept, but use a somewhat more involved rendition. I hope this will encourage people to pay attention to older, neater, and simpler concepts by adapting them to this modern, messier, and more complicated world. I'm trying to use a more specific formulation to help people recognize that the old saws are not so irrelevant as they might have thought.

People know that they should not lie. However, few seem to believe that they should not accept lies and half-truths about someone or something just because they do not like him or it.

On Facebook, I have un-followed any number of friends who made it their missions to convert all their contacts to their political way of thinking. Although I liked them personally, I did not want to read their misleading presumptions, falsehoods, and half-truths, even if I sometimes agreed with their ultimate positions. Poorly constructed arguments (and graphic memes often are) may sway people emotionally (see Principle #8, *If an emotional message is swaying your opinion, try to understand the core belief...*), but they seldom survive logical analysis. People post graphic memes (because of their speed and eye-appeal) without realizing that, while their emotional arguments may garner attention, they also may be doing a great deal of damage to logical inquiry, rational argument, and an over-arching belief in truth.

For many people, "Winning" (or at least feeling that one is superior) has become more important than "Truth".

At a time when appearing in a newspaper almost automatically guaranteed legitimacy, people used to warn, "Don't believe everything you read in the newspaper." In today's messy world, you could easily extend that to: "Don't believe every meme you read online." Nevertheless, the instant effect of the graphic meme is attractive because it often bypasses the slower, more logical efforts of the human mind. Many people, it seems, are loathed to relinquish the use of clever, if misleading, memes because refusing to use them would be sacrificing an effective intellectual (often a pseudo-intellectual) weapon.

Graphic memes are like political cartoons. If the newspaper favors one side of an argument, a talented cartoonist creates an exaggerated graphic image that will drive the newspaper's point home. This kind of exaggeration is expected in a cartoon since all cartoons exaggerate both appearance and the behavior of things. So, a cleverly conceived political cartoon can "argue" a point more effectively because it can engage the vision and make a joke at the same time. Look up "famous political cartoons" on the Internet to better understand this idea.

Graphic memes are also like bumper stickers. They summarize a concept in so succinct a manner that it is hard to disagree, at least without a pause for concentrated reasoning that does not easily occur while in traffic. Both an on-bumper sticker and an online meme are easy to remember and are made more memorable when jazzed up by an image that is intended to be emblematic of the argument (but often is itself biased, and/or does not actually come from the event that prompted the meme).

Do you remember the bumper sticker "If you think education is expensive, try ignorance"? Not a terribly controversial or political sentiment, it would appear. Who in his right mind would be against education? It seemed clever and also seemed to imply that some idiot somewhere must be lodging a movement against the school system, or perhaps the cost of state colleges. If you constantly saw the bumper sticker in daily life, you may have developed a predisposition toward public education no matter the cost to the local or state budget. You may have put no further thought into the matter. The meme is so powerful that it convinces without your considering any research or discussion. However, most memes are not well-formed arguments but clever partial arguments. Stop for a moment and think. Would you accept the value of an education if you had to pay for an overly expensive private school? Is education really the opposite of ignorance? Isn't knowledge the opposite of ignorance? Does education guarantee knowledge? Doesn't educational success depend on a student wanting to seek knowledge? Is knowledge the same thing as intelligence? Isn't intelligence what we really would like students to have? Does acquiring intelligence have to be expensive?

A counterargument can seldom take the form of a graphic meme. To be effective, a counterargument has to be spelled out. This spelling-out neither comports to contemporary culture's preferred speed, nor fits on a bumper, and thus these counterarguments tend not to become as popular or as convincing as the original bumper stickers or online memes.

In the years (perhaps decades) prior to writing this book, I have found that the Left was willing to believe any distortion of which the Right was accused, and the Right reciprocated the favor. We could argue which side was most egregious in this habit, or which initiated this sort of misleading emotional exhibition, but that is not my purpose here—both sides have been guilty. No matter which side of the aisle holds political power at the time, my Facebook friends have made emotional meme arguments for two reasons: (1) obviously because they are impassioned, but also (2) because a few people would bother reading a longer, more reasoned argument. (I would be willing to wager that my friends themselves would not be patient enough to read a longer, more reasoned argument, which is why the emotional shortcut was so appealing to them in the first place.)

Their tactics resulted in my posting a graphic of my own that many people LIKED…that is, before they returned to espousing their own causes while ignoring the truths this meme presents. *(N.B: Various versions of this graphic exist on the Internet. I obtained the one below indirectly on Facebook. Also note that a more extensive view of common fallacies appears in the appendix.)*

The Ten Commandments of Logic

1. Thou shalt not attack the person's character, but the argument. *(Ad hominem)*

2. Thou shalt not misrepresent or exaggerate a person's argument in order to make it easier to attack. *(Straw man fallacy)*

3. Thou shalt not use small numbers to represent the all. *(Hasty generalisation)*

4. Thou shalt not argue thy position by assuming one of its premises is true. *(Begging the question)*

5. Thou shalt not claim that because something occured before, it must be the cause. *(Post hoc/False cause)*

6. Thou shalt not reduce the argument down to two possibilities. *(False dichotomy)*

7. Thou shalt not argue that because of our ignorance, a claim must be true or false. *(Ad ignorantum)*

8. Thou shalt not lay the burden of proof onto him that is questioning the claim. *(Burden of proof reversal)*

9. Thou shalt not assume "this" follows "that" when there is no logical connection. *(Non sequitur)*

10. Thou shalt not argue that because a premise is popular, therefore it must be true. *(Bandwagon fallacy)*

I would argue that few human beings these days fully understand the value of logic, and fewer still know how it works. Aristotle would be ashamed of us. However, there are still a few of us who, when confronted with a meme or a set of political talking points, can take them apart logically.

Please understand, by the way, that a poorly constructed argument (i.e. one that commits errors of logic) does not mean that the *position* for which it argues is false; rather, it means that specific argument should be considered unconvincing (see "The Fallacy Fallacy" in the appendix). If there exists an objective truth about a topic, that truth exists without anyone arguing for it; but if a person wants to both *convince* another person of its veracity and *prove* the validity of a position (i.e., link the assertion to reality), an error-free logical argument is nearly impossible to beat. I say *nearly* impossible because, as of this writing, emotional arguments have likely earned more convinced adherents than logical arguments. Unfortunately, for the society in which we live, an emotional argument *convinces* far better than it *proves*. It wins followers who want to win arguments, not those who want to discover the truth. **In a war of words, there may be winners and losers, but often both sides wound the truth in the process.**

REASON CRITIQUED?

Ever since Immanuel Kant's *A Critique of Pure Reason* (1781), the idea of an objective truth has been on the decline. It has become more and more obvious that people tend to see things through their own set of fogged goggles and, as a result, your "truth" may not be mine. This, of course, perverts the meaning of "truth". More than a century later, Einstein's Special Relativity (1905) and General Relativity (1915) gradually came to be accepted by science. With no idea what Einstein meant, the common person in an attempt not to lose an argument, would offer, "Well, everything is relative" as a counter. It was a way of "agreeing to disagree". One would hope, however, that disagreeing parties would keep an eye on the facts and the results of their positions to determine if, in fact, either was correct. That "correctness" is measured by what happens. And that, in turn, implies that both parties are capable of seeing the same reality. You cannot argue that individual points of view must exist. However, emphasizing that there is no objective reality (as if no two people could ever see things the same way) is not only unfortunate, but also dangerous. It means that what happens doesn't count, which in turn would mean that there is no way of determining *any* view of reality.

A refusal to accept the possibility of an objective truth means that we can no longer offer convincing argumentation. Einstein's arguments, far from being a subjective refutation of objective truth, used logic and verifiable predictions to prove his theory.

Any convincing argument could be, and has been, dismissed with "That's just your opinion." If we can no longer convince a person using logic and/or facts as mutually accepted arbiters, there can be no unbiased adjudicator. There can be no way to fairly "win" an argument or peacefully convert an opponent. If logically convincing someone no longer exists, then whenever *winning* matters to people, they are more likely to use tactics like intimidation or bullying, rather than facts, logic, or reason. To them, "winning" will become more valuable than finding "the truth".

In the second half of the twentieth century, a group of French thinkers, eventually called the Postmodernist Philosophers, notably Jean Baudrillard, Jean-François Lyotard, and Jacques Derrida (Michel Foucault is also often cited as an early postmodernist although he rejected the label), took this philosophical relativism to the extreme. I am not an expert on Postmodernism, but I have done my research. In order not to unfairly devalue every word of every postmodernist's writing, let me enter this caveat. First, Lyotard defined Postmodernism as "incredulity to meta-narratives". I interpret that as not taking "accepted" truths as absolutes, a concept I can easily support. I am sure that other Postmodernist statements like this would garner a thumbs-up from me. However, the overall relativistic tendency of Postmodernists would not, so when I speak of Postmodernism, I am concentrating on the qualities as outlined by the Encyclopedia Britannica: "Many postmodernists hold one or more of the following views: (1) there is no objective reality; (2) there is no scientific or historical truth (objective truth); (3) science and technology (and even reason and logic) are not vehicles of human progress but suspect instruments of established power; (4) reason and logic are not universally valid; (5) there is no such thing as human nature (human behavior and psychology are socially determined or constructed); (6) language does not refer to a reality outside itself; (7) there is no certain knowledge; and (8) no general theory of the natural or social world can be valid or true (all are illegitimate 'metanarratives')."

More than 200 years after Kant's philosophy, more than 100 after Einstein's physics, and more than 50 years after the Postmodernists were writing, social media has shown us how influential philosophical relativism has become. Simultaneously, social media has also begun to extinguish social civility. Because now everyone can have an equal chance to voice his/her opinion publically (albeit often anonymously), everyone feels his/her opinion is worth being voiced, as if everyone were a closeted Kant or Einstein. Because a person wants to be heard (as if expounding a public opinion were like appearing in the newspaper used to be), he or she publishes unskillful and uninformed opinions. When other people disagree (with or without rational arguments to support their position), the riposte can result in intellectual, scholarly brilliance such as, "You're free to state your idiotic opinion, but it's an opinion of an ignorant anal pore." Not exactly the Point/Counterpoint of an academic debate. I refer you to the first of The Ten Commandments of Logic: "Thou Shalt Not Attack the Person's Character."

As an example, let's say that I make an argument defending a point of view (e.g. "Squirrels gather nuts for the winter"), the truth of which you cannot deny, but you feel squirrelly about it and still want to believe it is untrue. A rational person would respect the strength of my common-knowledge statement and either work to find weak aspects in my observation, site several counterexamples where squirrel gather potato chips for the spring, or work to strengthen arguments for his/her own point of view (e.g., searching the Internet for species of squirrels that do not gather nuts or do not seclude themselves during the snowy season). Unfortunately, in today's messy world, you are more likely to label me with an unpleasant epithet, not caring whether it is accurate, but assuming that it must be accurate because you *want* it to be accurate ("Obviously," you type, "your arguments reveals you as a Squirrel-ist, assuming that all squirrels think and act alike! Furthermore, you must therefore hate rodents, and by extension, all animals, as is proven by the fact that you not only stereotype squirrels but also eat lamb. Those who hate animals must hate human beings since humans are animals, so I am clearly within my rights to publically deny you access to all restaurants." And since your Squirrel-ist epithet must be accurate, you hope that others support your labeling me, thus giving you strength in numbers. But, **all the support in the world does not make something right**, to paraphrase Booker T. Washington.

Sorry, I know you wouldn't do that, but just pretend. Put yourself in the position of the person who denies the validity of my argument. If you do not accept logic and facts as valid moderators, with what tools would you counter my argument? I submit that you would be obliged to use either *ad hominem* arguments, contortions of my position, or outright lies.

Conversely, if you refuse to tell such lies (as per Principle #1), you are committing yourself to honoring the objective truth—or as close as you can come to it—rather than the subjective tactics of rage, smear, or mendacity.

Back in the days of the VHS cassette, I received a call at home from a martial artist who wanted to come to my *dojo* (school) to buy a video I was marketing. I told him, whenever he was ready, to give me a call in advance and I would have it for him. He showed up unannounced at my dojo one evening. I explained that the videos were stored at my home, but that if he could wait until after class, he could follow me home—a 6-minute drive—and I would be happy to get the video for him. No, he wasn't going to wait, and he departed.

Months later, when some false rumors about me surfaced on an Internet martial arts forum, he was one of the commenters who piled up against me. Why? He did not know me, had never witnessed a complete class, and could have no indication of the veracity or falsity of the claims. I can only assume that he was still annoyed at not obtaining the videocassette he wanted when he wanted it. The false rumors had nothing to do with the video, so no facts could be marshaled to support the rumor, but he wanted to "inconvenience" me, as he had allegedly been inconvenienced. The truth didn't matter. He also knew that the more negatives were piled up against me, the more likely people, unable to separate relevant argument from angry assertion, would believe the initial claim.

People are also more willing to accept false or severely biased statements about their side as *long as they are positive*. We tend to assume that, since we have great faith in our personal intuition, our side must be the more positive side. In the field of psychology, this is called the Dunning–Kruger effect. This is a cognitive bias in which a person of low ability or knowledge has an illusory sense of superiority and mistakenly assesses his/her cognitive ability as greater than it is. Sometimes, this bias occurs simply because an intolerant or annoyed person is looking for an enemy, i.e. someone to whom they can feel morally superior. I would argue that the willingness to accept negatives about the "other side", and false positives about their own, is also because people are more eager to join a side, a cause, a party, etc. so that side will think for them (see Principle #6: *Support, Don't Join*). In this way, they do not have to worry about researching each issue, and can feel ethically superior, all with a single decision to join.

Those people that identify with the political Right tend to watch FOX. Those that identify with the political Left tend to watch CNN or MsNBC. There is no PNN (Politically Neutral Network) from which to get perspective from both sides. In attempt to get the unvarnished news as well as astute insight, I have taken to watching a little CNN, paying close attention to the guests on the Right when they appear, and then to watching FOX panel discussions, paying close attention to the Left pundits. The network whose hosts and guests avoid groundless assertions and make reasonable arguments most, I will watch for the next few months, again paying special attention to the minority voices. The more I witness a moderator on one network espouse groundless accusations or avoid the use of logic, the less often I will tune into that program. The more programs like this a network offers, the less often I will watch that network—at least until the alternative network does the same thing.

But, it is not just politics! We all have our preferences in art, literature, music, etc. Don't we say, "I like Monet", for example, with our minds on the panoply of cathedral images painted at different times of the day, while ignoring much less interesting earlier paintings? Don't we really mean, "I like the majority of the mature works of Monet"? "Liking Monet" is an understandable kind of generalization, to be sure. Now, let's assume a friend of yours says, "I absolutely *hate* Monet. He is so bland and insipid. Seurat is much more interesting." Wouldn't you be shocked, not only at his judgment, but also at his reasoning? You show him a beautiful late Monet to change his mind, but he claims that "This may be beautiful, however it is not a late Claude Monet, but a less-well-known Georges Seurat!" In other words, having made a summary judgment based on his personal taste, he will not accept any evidence to the contrary, claiming that all contrary evidence cannot be valid since it does not agree with his own indisputable and thus perfectly valid taste!

Art, of course, is indeed subject to personal tastes, but we now live in a world so messy that the standards by which we judge art (and they are very subjective) are the standards by which we judge any position or point of view. No fact, no logical argument, or any other sort of attempt at objectivity is even considered.

IT GOES BOTH WAYS

If we should not believe lies about the "other side" just because we want them to be true, it stands to reason that we *should* believe provable facts about "our side" even if we wanted them to be false.

I recently saw a clever political survey that showed images of four high-priced mansions. An interviewer asked college students, all of which favored candidate X, which of these expensive homes belonged to six of the current candidates. The interviewer was careful not to bias the simple question, but allowed the students to set the standards by which they would judge. They all chose candidates Y, Z, YY, ZZ, and XYZ, but none chose their favorite, candidate X. When informed that *their* candidate, someone who had never emphasized personal income and allegedly stood for more income equality, owned *all* four of the homes, each student revised his/her opinion of the candidate. Given the students' values, I think their revisions were honest and appropriate. This is a clever and respectful way to bring back into reality, albeit slowly and in a piecemeal fashion, those opinions previously affected by hyperbolic rhetoric, well-rehearsed appearance, and misinformation. It is a way to face facilely formed opinions with facts, and without contention and accusation.

In a similar survey, the interviewer asked students what they thought of quotes taken from a political address. The students assumed it was an address that had recently been in the news—one that been delivered by a candidate they did not favor. Each student had a negative opinion of the quotes. When told that the "negative" quotes were from a candidate whom they *did* favor, they at first said, "That can't be true!" but faced with cognitive dissonance, they began to realize that their previously assuming a favorite candidate had slanted their judgment without their actually understanding the issues at hand, and especially without their understanding the "other side".

To their credit, they all recognized their biased points of view. Of course, this doesn't mean they will change political affiliations or vote for another candidate, but it does encourage them to be more careful in assuming that their "side" had a monopoly on truth or on advancing their values.

CHIPPING AWAY AT THE TRUTH

Another way people "tell lies" about the other side is to chip away in a lawyerly fashion at reasonable, convincing arguments. This is an attempt to make you reframe your argument internally so that you will cast doubt on your own thinking. If we are to be precise in applying our principle to this tactic, we should state the corollary, "**Do not believe refutations of your arguments when they are supported by exceptions and statistics that you cannot verify.**"

As the old saying goes, there are lies, damn lies, and statistics. Whenever someone sites a statistic, unless it is a very simple and easily verified, I immediately question his/her argument. There are so many ways that statistics are misused, it would be difficult to list them all, but I will offer some typical examples.

Stated statistic: 1% of all taxpayers hold 50% of all the money in circulation. Usually a statistic like this is used to show how unfairly income is distributed in the country or how a small number of citizens keep money to themselves that could flow to lower income citizens.

Problem #1: In any creative endeavor (including earning money) a very small percentage of the participants will always earn a disproportionately larger percentage of the profits (whether they be awards, praise, fame or income). This is called the Pareto Principle.

Problem #2: Assuming the statistic is accurate, one has to ask how fluid the membership of the 1% is. When first reading the statistic, you might assume that the 1% never changes, however it is more likely that most of the members of that 1% will not remain there. Similarly, members of the lowest income group may not remain there for long. The statistic may stay the same, but the people it allegedly represents do not.

Problem #3: Even if the membership of the 1% were not fluid, the "holding" of the money probably is. In other words, the dollars go out in expenditure and investment as quickly as they come in. Both expenditure and investment benefit those not in the 1%, which is a fact that counters the original intent of the stated statistic.

Here are some other ways statistics can go wrong (from *Wikipedia*):

Discarding unfavorable data

Another term related to this concept is cherry picking.

Loaded questions

The answers to surveys can often be manipulated by wording the question in such a way as to induce a prevalence towards a certain answer from the respondent. For example, in polling support for a war, the questions:

• Do you support the attempt by the USA to bring freedom and democracy to other places in the world?

• Do you support the unprovoked military action by the USA?

Overgeneralization

Overgeneralization is a fallacy occurring when a statistic about a particular population is asserted to hold among members of a group for which the original population is not a representative sample.

For example, suppose 100% of apples are observed to be red in summer. The assertion "All apples are red" would be an instance of overgeneralization because the original statistic was true only of a specific subset of apples (those in summer), which is not expected to be representative of the population of apples as a whole.

Biased samples

Scientists have learned at great cost that gathering good experimental data for statistical analysis is difficult. Example: The placebo effect (mind over body) is very powerful. 100% of subjects developed a rash when exposed to an inert substance that was falsely called poison ivy while few developed a rash to a "harmless" object that really was poison ivy. Researchers combat this effect by double-blind randomized comparative experiments. Statisticians typically worry more about the validity of the data than the analysis. This is reflected in a field of study within statistics known as the design of experiments.

Misreporting or misunderstanding of estimated error

If a research team wants to know how 300 million people feel about a certain topic, it would be impractical to ask all of them. However, if the team picks a random sample of about 1000 people, they can be fairly certain that the results given by this group are representative of what the larger group would have said if they had all been asked....

Many people may not realize that the randomness of the sample is very important. In practice, many opinion polls are conducted by phone, which distorts the sample in several ways, including exclusion of people who do not have phones, favoring the inclusion of people who have more than one phone, favoring the inclusion of people who are willing to participate in a phone survey over those who refuse, etc. Non-random sampling makes the estimated error unreliable.

False causality

If the number of people buying ice cream at the beach is statistically related to the number of people who drown at the beach, then nobody would claim ice cream causes drowning because it's obvious that it isn't so. (In this case, both drowning and ice cream buying are clearly related by a third factor: the number of people at the beach).

Confusing statistical significance with practical significance

Statistical significance is a measure of probability; practical significance is a measure of effect. A baldness cure is statistically significant if a sparse peach-fuzz usually covers the previously naked scalp. The cure is practically significant when a hat is no longer required in cold weather and the barber asks how much to take off the top.

Data manipulation

Informally called "fudging the data," this practice includes selective reporting and even simply making up false data.

Examples of selective reporting abound. The easiest and most common examples involve choosing a group of results that follow a pattern consistent with the preferred hypothesis while ignoring other results or "data runs" that contradict the hypothesis.

Neither tell nor believe lies about "the other side" just because you want them to be true.

2.

TRUTH:

Dare to be scrupulously honest even if it means losing—winning via a lie will gradually destroy you and
your cause, as well.

Scrupulous honesty, like scrupulously maintaining
any characteristic, is a pretty tall order. What is "scrupulous-
ness" anyway? The dictionary informs us that it has something to do with being *honorable* and *conscientious*. These
are the two characteristics I like to keep in mind when I try to
be as honest as possible in a messy world. Scrupulous honesty does not mean absolute, rigid honesty no matter what (as
we shall see below), but it does mean deferring to honesty as
a default position in normal circumstances, knowing that dishonesty is likely to foul up your own little niche of the world
and also contribute to how poorly the world functions.

"*Dare* to be honest..." suggests that most people do
not dare to do so because it is often easier to lie; they don't
dare to be honest because they are afraid to lose; or they
don't dare because they would rather gain a benefit in the
short-term than contribute to their own long-term wellbeing.

Doesn't "dare to be scrupulously honest" encompass the first principle "neither tell nor believe lies about the other side"? Kinda, sorta yes, although your honesty does not assume someone else's: "Dare to be scrupulously honest even if it means losing" assumes that even if you are an honest person, you might "lose" because of someone else's dishonest actions or rhetoric. Unfortunately, in today's messy world, although honesty may still be the best policy in the long run and for the larger society, it may not seem to be, especially when many of the people around you gain short-term successes by practicing various shades of dishonesty. You can be as honest as Saint Teresa and still find yourself deceived or sabotaged by someone whom you trusted, whom you believed to be as honest as you. If honesty, albeit a good policy, has not prevented you from losing, you will be tempted to win dishonorably. An honest person may have to tolerate an unfair loss in order to remain honorable.

Honesty, far from being a tool that guarantees short-term success, guarantees only peace of mind. And (to be honest) while the dishonest guy is winning, your scrupulous honesty may not even guarantee your peace of mind! You may never get to see how your counterpart's dishonesty, if not corrected, gets him/her pretty well pummeled personally (i.e. psychically and *vis-á-vis* a negative reputation), and may even cripple or crush his cause (i.e. his business, political party, movement, etc.)

For me, peace of mind is value enough, but for many people, serenity seems but a paltry benefit when looming and large are the other guy's profits from fraud, duplicity, and pretense.

WHY LIE?

Fresh out of college, I was employed at a summer program for a private school that hired newly graduated college students to teach elective courses. One of the art teachers was an attractive young woman whom I wanted to know. She told me that, during the school year, she taught at Milton Academy where her younger sister attended, that her father was in India at present, and that the sisters communicated with him via Ham radio. She was mature, beautiful, and intelligent—just my type of partner. Through a series of tiny inconsistencies, I was able to put together that her father was not in India nor did she use a Ham radio to communicate with him or anyone else. Then, I discovered that she did not teach at Milton Academy, but was a student enrolled in the very school where we were both now teaching. The ice cap on this little mountain of deceit was that, although she looked twenty-one, she was only sixteen years old! She could easily have gotten me into real trouble. I asked her directly why she had lied. "Life is more exciting that way," was her simple, unselfconscious reply.

Her trying to live out a fantasy life could easily have gotten me fired and could have put me in a tenuous position legally. Sure, hers was a youthful indiscretion, but her lying was a habit that, if uncorrected, might not only hurt others, but also result in her first being hired and then summarily fired without the benefit of a positive reference for future jobs. Negative reputations are hard to overcome.

You can tell yourself that you can still be *relatively* virtuous by being only a tiny bit dishonest while the rest of the world deals out more egregious treacheries. Most of us, I think, are "relatively" honest and that seems to suffice to get us through life. However, in the current messy world, even relative honesty, even tiny dishonesties that many people might ignore are becoming eclipsed by medium- and large-sized dishonest behavior that people willingly overlook. (At least that is my honest perception.) Honesty as the default standard seems to have lost its cachet. Journeying through a world in which a certain low level of lying or cheating is considered uncorrupt or at least unimportant, we need a hard turn toward scrupulous honesty, before a cliff appears.

How many people cheat, just a little, on their income tax returns? And who is to say what constitutes the fine line between legitimate, if slightly exaggerated, deductions and tax fraud? I would argue that, over the years, personal income tax has been responsible for lowering the scrupulous honesty of the majority of citizens. Certainly, there have been other factors, as well; but, focus for a moment on the mechanism of income taxes and, regardless of your feelings about them, try to understand my point.

The government needs money to fund programs that congress feels are beneficial. It levies taxes-on-earnings that are withdrawn weekly from a person's pay to make sure the person doesn't spend all his income before the government extracts its "take". Already, the person feels put upon. Sure, some people feel the government is serving them well and are happy to contribute their "fair share", but others feel that their share is not fair at all and that the government shouldn't be allowed to earn interest on money that, without income tax withholding, would have secured interest for the real earner. In either case, the earner does not want to give *more* than his/her fair share, so he/she tries to find a legal way to avoid a tax burden. Even if you fall into the "government can do no wrong" camp, you can see the incentive to fib a little on a tax return or hide some personal revenue. In this way, income tax gives even an honest person the incentive to be less than scrupulously honest. Accountants and tax specialists crop up to help preserve earnings, thus *costing* the earner money in order to save his/her money from an entity that didn't earn it, and so that, in filing his/her own tax return, the earner will not accidentally tell an untruth—a mistake that could cost him even more.

What about submitting a *curriculum vitae* or résumé for a job? No one has ever exaggerated or lied on one of those! Applicants tend to lean toward slight dishonesty because they know that other applicants will be even more severe in their deceptions.

As a senior in college, I applied for a teaching position that would begin in the fall, after graduation. I interviewed well, and finding myself in the list of finalists, I was brought back for a second interview. The first time around, the interviewer had asked me about my role as an Assistant Resident Counselor during my senior year. There was one ARC in every suite of 8 to 16 students. We were there as a resource for students who needed help emotionally or in any other way, and we were supposed to refer those students to the Senior Resident Counselor, one of which lived in each dorm.

During my first interview for the teaching job, I was asked how much actual counseling I had done. The question was impossible to answer since, although I talked with my suite-mates all the time, often visiting their rooms as any friend would, I had never formally sat down with a suite-mate who was complaining about life, studies, or a girlfriend. That was the job of the senior counselors. I tried to make that clear to my interviewer, but the question came up again in my second interview. It became obvious that the interviewer was on my side and was encouraging me to invent an unverifiable estimate of hours-on-the-job as a counselor. I could easily have said, "Oh, about four hours a week," and no one would have been able to check the veracity of my estimate. The interviewer tried three times to get an erroneous estimate from me, but I would not lie or invent facts even though it would have enhanced my application. Someone else got the job.

What about a little fib to enhance your reputation or status? I had a karate student (we'll call him Otto) who, like several other black belt holders, taught beginners in a separate room while I instructed the main class. One day, we had guests from another school walk in the dojo while I was teaching my class. Otto had finished his beginner class and, along with another student who was at the desk, properly welcomed in the guests. Otto took over the duties as host, introduced himself by name, and said, "I teach here with Tony." He did not use the more appropriate "Sensei Annesi", nor did he make clear that he taught beginners only a few times each year. Cleverly telling the literal truth, he misled the guests in order to gain their attention and raise his status. Unfortunately, I overheard him from the main mat and Otto's status immediately dropped in my personal assessment. So, to feel better about himself by impressing others, Otto accidentally made a negative impression on his teacher who should have mattered more to him than that evening's guests.

That little circumnavigation, although not an outright lie, made me wary of him for the rest of our relationship.

In a similar incident, I met a fellow karate instructor (I'll call him Seth) at a tournament. In our conversation, Seth mentioned that he had gone to Okinawa and trained at the dojo of the person who had founded his art fifty years before. Obviously, he did not know karate history as well as I (or assumed that I did not know history very well). That now deceased founder never owned a dojo—he had taught in his backyard. The truth was that Seth had studied for a week in the dojo of one of the founder's senior students. Assuming incorrectly that the dojo had originally belonged to the founder, he turned a reasonable bragging right into a deceitful bragging right. I put the incident aside since anyone could have made that erroneous assumption, but then he went further. Seth and I both knew a very senior local martial artist who was the first person to teach this same art in the USA (I'll call him Master T). Seth informed me that he had "gotten" Master T his eighth degree black belt. That vague statement seemed disingenuous at best, since Seth was a much lower rank and had no way, as far as I could tell, to influence the more senior officials on Okinawa. I wondered for a moment if he had put in a good word for Master T, but I knew that a recommendation from a junior black belt would not be a valid reason for the Okinawan masters to promote Master T. Weeks later, I visited Master T and discovered that Seth's "getting" Master T's eight degree black belt for him meant only that he had physically transported the certificate from Okinawa. Seth had used a vague statement in order to deceive me (and probably others) to think of him as both an accomplished and influential martial artist. It did just the opposite. I avoided any dealings with him from that time forward.

MAINTAINING HONOR

As battle lines are drawn in everyday society (Left vs. Right, Socialism vs. Capitalism, Women vs. Men, Resistance vs. Tolerance, Activism vs. Patience, Experimentation vs. Tradition, etc.), dishonesty has become more easily justifiable in the minds of the dedicated advocate. After all, the only time it is virtuous to lie, cheat, and steal is during wartime, and then only to hurt the enemy. In this messy world, those who simply disagree with people of a certain disposition are too often considered "the enemy". As soon as disagreement becomes opposition and opposition becomes enmity, one side or the other (often both) will feel it is acceptable to destroy its enemy by dishonest means—means that it would never have considered if the "enemy" were only a "competitor". That's why my first principle is: "Neither tell nor believe lies about 'the other side' just because you want them to be true."

So if we cannot overcome the desire to see an opponent as an enemy, either because we do not know how to overcome our own emotions or because the opponent keeps escalating the emotional impact and costs of the disagreement, then we must at least dare to be scrupulously honest. If we lose the prize while daring to be honest, we set an example that is unassailable both in our own minds and in the minds of those who know us well. We might even influence someone else to do the same. We might even impress someone who is important to us that we had the guts to sacrifice a short-term gain for the sake of honesty. Honesty has the same root in Middle English as does the word Honor. "Honest" means, "held in honor, or deserving of honor".

Nearing the end of his years, a very senior martial artist I knew wanted to pass his art down to one of his students, and he wanted the transmission of leadership to be publically recognized so that no one could challenge its authenticity. Both the senior martial artist and his proposed inheritor attended the annual convention of a "martial arts recognition council" of which I was a part. As it happened, the inheritor was two years younger than the council's minimum age for a recognized heir. The senior martial artist on one hand and a few members of the council on the other were trying their best to bend the rules to allow the certification. I took the proposed inheritor aside and suggested that his inheritance was going to happen whether or not the council recognized it, so why not back off, politely honor the council's rules, and simply reapply in two years. He and his teacher took this advice.

The proposed inheritor had relieved the council of the pressure to break its own rules in order to satisfy the respected senior instructor, and the council saw it as an honorable act since it relinquished a short-term gain. The potential inheritor had been conscientious enough to sacrifice the council's recognition in order to allow the council to maintain its honor. Sure, the easy way out would simply have been to lie about his age, but because of his action, no one needed to make an exception and no one needed to twist truths—no one needed to lie about either rules or qualifications.

We have all run into deceitful opponents. Lying opponents can lie about us then lie that they lied, but our knowing that our characters are upright allows us to play a longer game. Should the longer game not be available to us, we can take solace in the idea that the lying antagonists in our lives, should they not correct their ways, will not be able to play the long game, either. We retain our positive character while they take the chance of earning a negative reputation. They might get the job, but someone will eventually discover that they were only a sixteen-year-old student and a chronic and habitual liar.

Of course, there is no absolute guarantee that the deceitful or dishonest people among us will not retire old, rich, and famous. It happens. It also happens that many virtuous people die unrewarded. Still, I suspect that there is an important cultural tipping point that shifts the balance, no matter if a society is going upward or downward. If it is true, as I suggest, that we live in an increasingly messier world because we have ignored many centuries of accumulated and refined ethical standards (ethical standards from religions, from folk wisdom, from business, and even from personal improvement practices like the traditional martial arts), it is also true that we can tip society's balance toward order (or at least un-messiness) by staying as honest as possible at all times, even if we occasionally lose.

If we are willing to use untruths to avoid losing, we will find ourselves the vanquished as often as the victor, and we will not know whom to trust in a world that will end up so messy that Washington, D.C. will look like Mount Everest.

The short and simple way of saying this might have been: "The end does not justify the means." Well, of course not! But I suspect that in today's messy world, increasingly fewer people accept this aphorism as a truth or as a guideline. Until a vast majority of us takes an assessment of our own behavior and willfully self-corrects, the tipping point that will change society toward honesty as a default position will always seem too far away.

DEFENSIVE DECEIT

What about lying to advance a larger cause? This might be an instance of a larger more important end justifying the smaller, rather insignificant means, for example, by perpetrating a lie that no one would notice. I realize that this can be a knotty problem.

At the risk of conjuring up a modern-day version of a scene from *The Brothers Karamazov*, imagine a doubting parishioner, who is struggling with his faith, asking a priest if he absolutely knows God exists. Father Alyosha certainly believes God exists, otherwise he would not be a priest; but he cannot say he knows for certain that God exists. If he answers, "Yes, I know for certain," he would be lying, thus sinning before the God he believes exists, but if he answers, "No, I do not know for certain," he may contribute to the further loss of his parishioner's faith, thus failing in his duty as a priest. Most of us, if put in Alyosha's position, would reframe the question (more on Reframing in Principle #3 below) in order to give an honest answer: "Well, I must admit that I cannot offer definitive assurance that God exists, but I feel as strongly as one can feel that He does." Nice sidestep, Father. He didn't ask about your feelings, he asked about your knowledge. You managed not to lie and still honestly convey your conviction.

Now, what if the parishioner, rather than being in a crisis of faith, were in a crisis of sanity? What if he were wearing an explosive vest in the middle of a crowded church and would press the bomb's trigger unless the priest could say that he absolutely knows that God exists? Wouldn't the priest tell a lie in order to save all the other people in the church? I think he would. I call this Defensive Deceit.

Defensive Deceit is when you mislead in order to protect yourself from those who maliciously deceive, or are trying to relieve you of property, time, effort, or in the extreme, your life. Defensive Deceit is related to striking back in kind. A DD action is not perpetrated upon anyone, but is activated only when some nemeses attempts to take advantage of you. It is like counterpunching because some-one punched first.

I am afraid there is no way to avoid punching back someone that constantly punches or attempts to punch you, unless you wish to be a pacifist, a punching bag, and/or a martyr. As a martial artist, I know that courts would treat me as a special case if I struck someone, even in self-defense, but if some delusional dude decided to duke it out with me and I could not escape the encounter, I would avoid his blows as much as possible and then deck him even if he con-sistently missed his target. I would argue that, if his blows had connected and I had been hurt, I might not have been able to keep him from continuing his rampage.

Picture a home invader asking you at gunpoint if there is any hidden money in the house that you occupy alone. Would you lead him to your wall safe that held the money to pay for your daughter's operation? Most of us would hold that there is no moral obligation to tell the truth to someone who is threatening you.

Defensive Deceit might be excusable, but we should seriously think about Defensive Deceit bleeding into the less dramatic aspects of our lives. It is not unusual that we use "white lies" to protect ourselves from those whose goals seem more nefarious. Have you ever put a sticker on your car or home window, warning a potential thief that there is an active alarm system when you never actually installed the system? Does your phone message explain that you are not at home when, in reality, you are just screening your calls? Do you have a timer on your living room lamp and TV to deceive potential burglars into believing that someone is there, when you are, in fact, out to dinner? Have you ever invented an invisible secretary or private assistant that callers or e-mailers have to pass through in order to talk to you personally? One could easily argue that in these cases, you have not been scrupulously honest! You, in turn, might argue that you are practicing Defensive Deceit, that no one will be hurt by your duplicity, and that your deceit would be unnecessary if there were no "enemies" at the door. In other words, those who would take advantage of your time and money have put you into a minor war with the nemeses of daily life. I am not here to cast moral aspersions on those who practice Defensive Deceit, knowing how difficult it is to be free of nemeses who wish to take advantage of your honesty or good nature, but I would like to see more people use creativity to avoid even this sort of dishonesty, if possible.

Advertisers are creative in this way. They know what sells. They can tell you, for example, that people are often attracted by the new and different. Therefore companies seem to "renew" their products on a regular basis. But advertisers cannot legally call something new that is not new, can they? That would be the type of lying called "false advertising". They ask themselves, "How can we creatively and legally get around that?" I have an idea! Lobby the Federal Trade Commission to make it legal to label as NEW any product or aspect of a product that is at least 20% changed. That is the current standard, by the way, and one of the reasons we have so many different versions of an otherwise commonplace product.

Why do car models change their designs yearly? It's because if they weren't at least 20% new, you wouldn't buy the new model.

Still can't make a 20% change? Create a new *brand* manufactured by the same parent company. It is literally "brand new", but its content may be only 5% different from another item produced by the same company under a different name—creativity to the rescue.

Advertisers cannot lie outright about their products or service if they want to avoid being sued or fined. Instead, they use their creativity, emphasizing some positive aspect of what they offer, thus they ethically *redirect* to avoid the need to unethically *mislead*. For example, they may not have the *most popular* plumbing business in the metro area, but they have the fastest growing plumbing business (of the three existing plumbing businesses). They may not have the lowest *costing* rubber ducky in the toy store, but they have the one that kids *prefer* (in a recent survey done in a Bayonne nursery). You get the idea.

Instead of lying in your everyday interactions, dare to be creative thus circumnavigating the need to Defensively Deceive whenever possible. Using DD implies that you see the other party as a nemesis, so you might wish to be careful when using it with friends and acquaintances. Was Otto or Seth using Defensive Deceit? No, although they did not literally lie, their deceit was more offensive because they were not trying to counteract someone who was out to deceive or trap them. Neither the guest at my dojo nor I were their nemeses.

I am sure the several women I had met on an on-line dating site thought they were using DD when they said that they would write tomorrow or told me on the phone, "we'll talk soon." No messages or calls did I receive from them nor any responses to my attempts to reach out. "Ghosting" is not really DD; it's just rude.

Avoiding minor deception can take some effort. For many people, that effort to avoid deception does not seem to be worthwhile since what is at stake is not the loss of a war, a battle, or even a job! True, but creativity in avoiding deception gives you practice in scrupulous honesty, and that honesty both helps your reputation and, if it were to become a culturally accepted premise, your willingness to trust others, as well. Also, in the same way that experienced consumers recognize when an ad is avoiding one claim to emphasize another, the average person will likely recognize when someone is applying creativity to avoid deception.

I did not haphazardly use "dare" as the first word in this guideline principle. If I am correct about the culture having become messier over time, veering away from baked-in values, then one can recognize the following cultural change in both truth and courage. It used to take daring to step over the line of truth into deception and then, in some cases, outright mendacity. Only the bad-asses among us had that daring. Since bad-asses dared to be different, as a culture, we gradually began to admire their courage. And then, since they were often successful, we imitated it. In this messy world, it will take just as much daring to veer toward truth and honesty.

Dare to be scrupulously honest even if it means losing—winning via a lie will gradually destroy you and your cause, as well.

3.

TRUTH:

Reframe the facts to make yourself feel better, if you like, but don't represent that reframe as the objective truth.

"Reframing" is a skill taught in Neuro-Linguistic Programming (NLP). Richard Bandler and John Grinder founded this self-development branch of psychotherapy in the early 1970s, deriving it, according to them, from the work of Virginia Satir, Milton Erickson, and Fritz Perls. Perhaps its most famous advocate was Tony Robbins.

NLP has many fascinating and useful tools for changing your attitude and view of life. For example, "reframing" is a technique that allows you to see a problem as an opportunity or a benefit. Let's say a policeman stopped you for driving 7.5 miles-an-hour over the speed limit. You could be disgruntled, mumbling to yourself that other people travel a lot faster in that area and *they* are never arrested. Alternatively, to avoid disgruntled-ness, you might simply "reframe" the situation like this: "Whew! Thank goodness that traffic officer stopped me! If he hadn't, I might have gotten into an accident with the car that just ran the stop sign at the next intersection." Sure, you don't know for certain if any car *really* ran the stop sign or if you would really have been in an accident, but if you were honest with yourself, you also don't know for certain that many other drivers escaped arrest when speeding in that area. By reframing your negative response so that it feels like a positive response, you change your attitude for the better.

I first began to investigate NLP because of a lecture my business roundtable group sponsored in the 1980s. I was fascinated by the simple and seemingly rapid methods of self-improvement that NLP offered. Once I listened to Tony Robbins' 1986 audio program *Unlimited Power*, I was sold.

Unfortunately, any tool can be misused and, over the years, I have seen friends, advertisers, and scads of politicians use reframing in a way that, I suspect, Bandler and Grinder had not intended.

A friend and student of mine reframed every occurrence that others might consider negative. *Their* negative perception of reality, after all, did not need to be her perception of reality. In my opinion, however, she overdid it, drifting into Polyanna-land. If caught in a typhoon, she would note how aesthetically the palm trees swayed. Okay, Ms. Polly, time to take shelter before that lovely typhoon uproots its swaying trunk and knocks your lovely trunk down to root level! Of course, that's just *my* reality, isn't it?

So, if each of us has his or her own reality, what then is the difference between opinion and reality? If we accept that there is no objective reality, and prefer to reframe what occurs into the consistently positive, won't the cold fact of being hit by a flying palm tree suggest otherwise? Or will we be forced to reframe our life-threatening injuries, too? The danger of over-reframing is willingly becoming unattached to the world.

I propose, in contradistinction to the postmodernist no-objective-reality dogma, that there is a bottom line of human nature that can be called "common normality". For example, people generally prefer life to death, pleasure to pain, and success to failure. If they did not, they would be failed, in pain, and dead in short order. Therefore, human beings can be said to share some basic characteristics. One subjective view of a situation can vary from another, of course, but the fundamentals do not.

Having been hit by a flying palm tree, you might want to see the positive side of a negative situation that you could not have avoided. For example, lying in the hospital while recovering would give you the opportunity to see who really cares about you; it could afford you the chance to study the efficiency of hospital regimen; or, it could allow you to have breakfast in bed every day. If you reframe a situation positively and it helps your attitude, *well good on ya, mate*; but if you present that subjective reframe as objective reality—something positive enough that you would not try to avoid it—you may be defying human nature, or at least "common normality". Is finding out who cares about you, studying hospital efficiency, or having breakfast in bed worth the concussion and the four broken ribs? Nobody thinks it is a good thing to get flattened by a flying tree! So painting your negative situation with a positive brush, while it may be good for your attitude, does not change the reality of the situation.

"But, I'm not changing the reality of the situation," you say, "I'm simply changing my evaluation of it." Agreed. So, would you do it again? If you believe that there is no objective reality, but that you "create" a subjective reality, why don't you try to walk out of the hospital and resume your life as if you were never injured? Are your broken bones a social construct or a collective illusion? *What is* and *how you see what is* are two different things.

I wrote above that "common normality" was in contradistinction to the postmodernist dogma. Now I would ask, "How can a group of people believe they collectively create their own reality and then expect the rest of us to also see things their way? After all, by their own admission, our reality is not theirs. Ironically, by presenting their subjective reality as objective reality, they are contradicting their own presumption that there is no objective reality.

Government officials have told lies to protect national security. Okay, let's recognize national security as a valid excuse to lie—a Defensive Deception. However, once citizens accept that excuse, a government can claim "national security" for any reason, thus having instant access to deceiving its own populace.

Often official government deceptions take the form of tweaks of the truth that have more to do with reframing than with direct lying. Euphemisms creatively reframe a common term. I admit that without euphemisms and their cousins hyperbole, simile, and metaphor, we could not have either advertising, song, or for that matter, creative literature. Often, however, those euphemisms are meant to hide what plainer terms could not hide.

What, for example, is "revenue enhancement"? It's common called taxation. It could be considered "enhancement" only from a governmental point of view. Your personal revenue is not enhanced by taxation. At the very mildest, from the taxpayer's point of view, it is revenue transfer. Similarly, the Internal Revenue Service (IRS) is indeed a service, but it does not serve the taxpayer—in fact, the taxpayer serves it. The IRS serves the government. Those "renames" are meant to reframe the minds of the taxpayer. They serve the government's desire for you to be comfortable with their collecting your money under the presumption that it will return services of equal value. But these euphemisms are not objective reality. Trying to portray these "renames" as objective reality are at least mild attempts at deception.

The above is admittedly a relatively innocuous example. What about more offensive examples like "ethnic cleansing" (genocide), "collateral damage" (innocents killed), "enhanced interrogation" (torture), or "extraordinary rendition" (kidnapping)? Okay, I understand how a military that uses plainer, more direct terms cannot come across as the artisans of justice-through-might, but those euphemisms nonetheless contribute to a messy society full of semi-truths (and thus semi-lies) instead of honesty.

What about rights? It used to be taken for granted that "rights" meant personal freedoms that governments or individuals could not deprive you of. The first ten amendments to the Constitution of The United States (The Bill of Rights) specify the limitations of government. Over my lifetime, people have gone from referring to individual rights to referring to group rights as if the groups were not made up of individuals. Women's Rights, for example, cannot be separate from individual rights because women are clearly individuals. No subdivision of individual rights is needed. However, since the argument was that many women were excluded from certain individual rights because they were women, the idea of Women's Rights took hold. Makes sense so far.

Then, the meaning of "rights" was stretched. Welfare Rights meant that those qualified for welfare should receive what the law had promised them, even if those benefits are not strictly rights. Housing rights? If a state or local government promised subsidized housing to all families under a certain income level and it reneged on that promise, welfare recipients, even though they were getting the benefits of other people's labors through government auspices, were not receiving what they had expected. Were their rights being taken away or were certain *privileges* being truncated?

Now we see the word "rights" attached to groups and causes that expect subsidies from either government or from someone else! The right to health, the right to work, and the right to security are all desires that have nothing to do with the state or any individual entity preventing you from working toward health, work, and security or maintaining the health, work, and security you already have. In this new interpretation of rights, human beings have an inherent entitlement to these things. At whose expense? Since these things are neither innate, nor growing in the common meadow, someone has to provide them. So the newly revised use of "right" implies taking away a "right" of someone else in order to satisfy a need or desire.

Jamie Whyte, in his book *Crimes Against Logic*, writes, "…when anyone claims a right, first ask which duties does this right impose on others; that will tell you what the right is supposed to be…. It will often be clear that no one really has the implied duties, or that it would be preposterous to claim they should." The reframing of common words like "right" has smuggled in meanings that have actually changed, and in some cases, inverted the meaning of those words. For this reason, I am against politically correct speech.

The original idea of PC speech was to avoid giving needless offensive to people who may have little cultural power. Okay, sounds polite, doesn't it? I'd support and encourage not using "crippled" but substituting "handicapped". We could easily ratchet that up from "handicapped" to "special needs" without hearing very much dissent from me. But let's not go to simply "special", thus conflating those who may need help with those who have well above average skills. It is one thing to avoid offending people and another to try to make them into something they are not—that would be intentional deception. Ironically, that reframe also begins to erase the very reason that the "handicapped" or "special needs" categorization was created in the first place, as if you could erase the reality of a recognized problem by promoting the notion that others should not perceive it. As such, it contributes to the messiness of the world.

ANOTHER REALITY?

A portion of our brain is known as the Reticular Formation (or the Reticular Activating System). "Reticular" means "net-like". It serves to bring to our attention items for which we have an interest. If you think you'd like to buy a Porsche, suddenly several models of Porsche seem to be passing by you every time you are driving. If you really enjoy barbecue, your attention will be pulled to the magazine on the rack that starts with BARB, even if it turns out to be about Barbie dolls. If you fear snakes, a dog leash dropped in the grass makes you jump before your eyes even notice that the dog and its owner are romping six feet in front of you.

People tend to see what they want to see, positive or negative. This means that in addition to reframing an event in order to feel more positive about it, people tend to reframe negatively when they have already prejudged the negativity of the situation or person. If they are predisposed to think badly of someone, they will see the bad this person does, or they will interpret the good she does as being done for a disreputable ulterior motive. Conversely, if they are predisposed to think well of someone, they will see her negative behaviors as having been misunderstood. In other words, people tend to judge first and interpret facts afterwards.

When they think they are being objective, they are often being as subjective as can be, having predetermined their point of view based on some bias or preference. This speaks to the idea held by postmodernist philosophers, that there is no objective reality, only subjective experience. No one can deny the existence of subjective experience. But what is that experience *based on*?

I remember a long conversation I had with a college professor whom I was considering dating. We shared our various points of view, each trying to understand how the other thought, and to be frank, I was gratified to know that she was intelligent, experienced, and could hold up her side of an intellectual conversation. Then, in relation to some topic we were discussing, she referred to there being no objective reality and I asked her to explain. She did not cite either Kant or the Postmodernists, but I probably could not have either, so I was waiting for some other basis for her belief. I was disappointed to discover that her certainty was based only on an Argument from Authority. She said, "It is widely accepted in academic circles that there is no objective reality. We each perceive things differently."

"Certainly that is true." I then asked, "But what is it that we are perceiving?" She could not answer and became indignant.

Objects in front of us may not look to you exactly the way they look to me—admittedly, that is something we can never know for sure—but when I ask you to pass the salt, you never kick off your shoes, dance on the table, then boot the gravy boat toward me. We understand each other. That understanding begins because we both perceive *something*. And that something must be similar enough to each of us so we can communicate about it. Even if you do not consider our mutually agreed upon definitions of objects and actions as evidence for objective reality, assuming that each of us invents his/her own reality would mean a heightened chance that no communication could take place. Therefore, nothing could be accomplished accept by a single person. We couldn't even salt our food, let alone send human beings to the moon.

In *Global Brain*, Chapter 7 "A Trip Through the Perception Factory", Howard Bloom discusses the concept of objective reality. He explains that in the 1920s and 1930s, The Logical Positivists held that knowledge was "sense-data" and that this data was "objective and unalterable". Counter to this position were The Radical Constructionists who claimed that reality was a fabrication of the mind. Bloom goes on to detail the complicated way in which our vision (in his example) takes in only a selected array of items and then filters those inputs even further. The results, he claims in the succeeding chapter, is that "reality is a shared hallucination".

His is a strong argument against "sense-data" as the equivalent of reality. Dogs and cats do not see the world as human beings do, and bugs do not perceive reality the way birds do because each has a different perceptual system and a different brain construction, thus each interprets given data with different senses. However, what this tells us is that perceptions can vary and that no paraphernalia of perception may be able to take in all of reality, therefore no one can know what true, all-inclusive reality is. *But that does not disprove that there is a reality to be known.* Further, when Bloom suggests that "reality is a shared hallucination", he is admitting that within human experience that "shared hallucination" *functions* as reality, like the "common normality" I referenced above. We may interpret what we experience differently and we may even recognize certain things and ignore others, but we *do not produce reality* as if we were demi-gods.

Bloom explains that social experience actually can shape a developing brain's physiology. Brain cells that are not employed to process the sights and sounds of a child's given cultural environment will actually die off, "biasing" the brain to readily accessible sights and sounds. We can understand, therefore, how everyone can develop his own point of view or his own language's accents, and how difficult it must be to experience reality the way someone else does.

Above I noted that people tend to see what they want to see, positive or negative. Alternately, people tend to see what they have been conditioned to see (as Bloom suggests). The attempt to reframe the perceptions of a populace is an attempt to condition the populace to see things differently. This is neither good nor bad in itself, but as with any tool, it can be used in ways that we might not prefer. You can use a knife to slice bread or to stab a fellow diner. The knife is a tool. So is reframing. It is up to the individual to be responsible in using that tool and to recognize when the tool is being used irresponsibly. No matter how conditioned you are to see something, short of a physiological or psychological abnormality, you will never see a knife used as either a gun or a glockenspiel. Even if you did, the knife will neither fire a bullet nor play a tune.

How do we "know" that people perceive things differently? We perform tests and perceive the results. If we really created our own realities, we could never agree that people see things differently since I could experience your test results as turnip soup or a tire iron and you could not argue about my perception since your test results tell you that you are perceiving the "true" reality—a reality that says there is no true reality.

Because people implicitly accept that they are unique individuals, they also embrace their own perceptions of reality. But that's a bit lonely for them. It also may even feel unsafe. So, understandably, they then associate with groups. In order to retain membership in that group, they adjust their individual perceptions, adopting the group's point of view. Referring once again to Howard Bloom's *Global Brain*, we discover that associating in groups is both natural and essential for survival. But membership must enforce conformity. In both animals and humans, members of the group will employ various methods, ranging from teasing to violence, to maintain the group's unanimity. Anyone who has lived through junior high school realizes that the remnants of this prehistoric survival mechanism are still alive. Bloom writes, "Conformity-enforcing packs of vicious children and adults gradually shape the social complexes we know as religion, science, corporations, ethnic groups, and even nations."

Bloom makes the point that there is a strong drive to conformity in many animal species such that if an animal is injured, the group usually shuns it. This probably is part of a survival mechanism: an injured member cannot keep up with the pack or cannot hold its own during a hunt, for example.

No stragglers needed or wanted. Over centuries, humans have created enough compensation mechanisms that there is a much wider tolerance for people who are sick, injured, or simply different. However, the tighter the group's focus, the less is the tolerance for diversity.

If a group becomes contentious to the extent that its *raison d'etre* is to oppose another group, its members will also see that other group, or members thereof, as malicious and dangerous. George Orwell said, "Public opinion, because of the tremendous urge to conformity in gregarious animals, is less tolerant than any system of law." In the above assessment, I would read "public opinion" as "group opinion".

Ironically, loneliness and the ancient drive for survival leads an individual to seek out a community. That community has its boundaries, thus it creates isolation from the rest of the world. Individuals feel they cannot survive either the group's restrictions or its isolation and break away to start the cycle again.

THE SHOE ON THE OTHER FOOT

Since it is true that we all see through our own eyes, we may think that spending half a moment estimating the view through someone else's eyes is the same as being objective. It is not. Truly seeing through someone else's eyes is, of course, impossible. Often our attempt to see, as if through someone else's eyes, is simply seeing through our own eyes from another direction. Sure, it gives us another perspective, but it doesn't shape that perspective with the unique biology, psychology, and history that the other person owns. What's worse is that we won't actually discover the other person's perspective. Instead, we will assume what the other person's perspective must be. In other words, we subjectively guesstimate their subjective point of view and consider ourselves objective.

The third of Don Miguel Ruiz's Four Agreements is "Don't Make Assumptions". He believes that with this single agreement with yourself, you can change your life. "Don't Make Assumptions" implies that, beyond being honest with ourselves, we have to make a sincere effort to understand what the other person intends and where he or she is coming from.

Here is part of a martial arts blog I wrote in 2018 entitled "Taking and Getting Perspective", reproduced in *Sunday with Sensei's Journal, Vol. 5: Preserve and Improve*.

As far as we know, humans are the only animals that can perform the amazing feat of mentally putting themselves into another being's situation. It is so natural to us, that we do it automatically regardless of whether our assumptions about that other being prove accurate or not. (For more on this and other perceptions regarding the minds of others, consider Nicholas Epley's *Mindwise*).

Romances break up because one party assumes that the other party must have meant A, when no, the other party meant Z. The temptation to believe one's own "wisdom" when attempting to *take another's perspective* is overwhelming. We confidently assume that the other party not only could not have meant Z, but we also assume the other party is now lying about it. Knowing that people lie to protect themselves, we assume that the other party *must* be lying because, after all, he/she clearly *must* have meant A. This circular argument invests us in our ability to *take* another person's perspective, and prevents us from *getting* that person's actual perspective.

To *get* (rather than take) perspective, one has to engage in honest conversation. If the conversation is likely to be awkward or if we assume the person is likely to lie, we avoid the very mechanism by which we can get the other person's true perspective.

There are other complicating factors, as well. Sometimes, the person in question is not fully conscious of whether he meant A, Z, or something in between. Sometimes, there are unknown factors that contribute to the person implying A but really meaning Z—factors he is keeping from you to protect, or even to serve you, the very person who is calling him a liar.

Here is a cartoon from Facebook that illustrates this point:

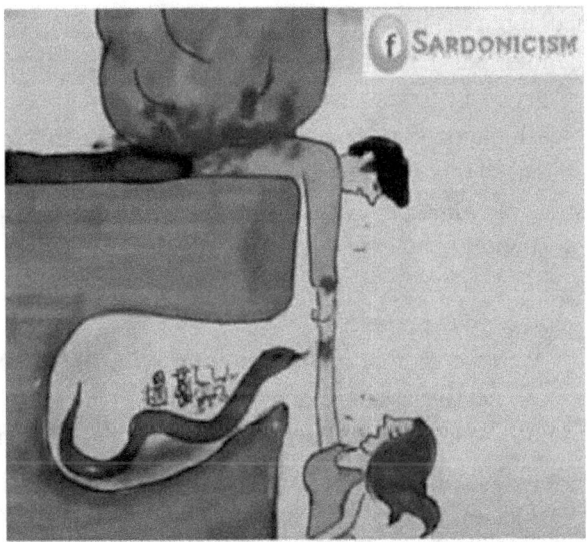

The man can't see the snake biting his wife, and the woman can't see the boulder on her husbands back, the moral of the story here is that sometimes a man can't see the pain his wife is suffering from and women can't understand the pressure men feel on a day to day basis, within couples we need to learn to understand each other more and communicate better so we can seek out the problems and turn weaknesses into strengths 🖤 💯

I can tell you of several romantic break-ups I have experienced after the woman assumed something of me that was not true. Having made the untrue assumption, anything I said to defend myself would not change her mind because, in her opinion, I was just defending my misbehavior, rather than having the character to admit I was wrong and apologize. Each of these women probably misjudged me because she was not used to having a scrupulously honest guy in her life. My having done something that reminded her of a previous occurrence, something about which she was sensitive, seemed to put me in "her other guy's shoes". Finding herself in a familiar place, she made a familiar assumption that may have proven true in the past. Instead of *getting* my perspective by asking me for clarification and engaging in a serious discussion, she *took* a perspective she thought was mine, fooling herself into believing that her subjective presumption, unsupported by evidence, must be objective truth. In other words, each woman made an assumption based on her own subjective experiences.

We *take* another person's point-of-view by using our own subjective assumptions. We tend to avoid *getting* their point-of-view because even within a seemingly honest discussion, we could not be sure of the other person's veracity. Thus, we become stuck in our own field of experience and judge others from there. The only way out of that field is not to *take* their point-of-view, but to walk in the other person's shoes for a while. Since that is often impractical, the next best way is to simply talk to him/her with a sincerely interested attitude, rather than an attitude so lowered by a previous negative experience that it prevents a ride on the objectivity elevator.

Disagreements, once established, will often lead to misunderstandings; but, initial misunderstandings lead to disagreements only when your emotional reaction makes you too proud of being the "injured party" to discover the truth.

Reframe the facts to make yourself feel better, if you like, but don't represent that reframe as the objective truth.

Re: TRUTH

"Never say anything about someone that you wouldn't say to them directly and don't try people without accusing them to their faces." — Ray Dalio

"When distant and unfamiliar and complex things are communicated to great masses of people, the truth suffers a considerable and often a radical distortion. The complex is made over into the simple, the hypothetical into the dogmatic, and the relative into an absolute." — Walter Lippmann

"Truth—or, more precisely, an accurate understanding of reality—is the essential foundation for any good outcome.... The biggest mistake most people make is to not see themselves and others objectively, which leads them to bump into their own and others' weaknesses again and again.... Successful people are those who can go above themselves to see things objectively and manage those things to shape change.... It requires you to replace your attachment to always being right with the joy of learning what's true."
— Ray Dalio

4.

COURAGE:

Dare to lose in love, in business, and in life—losing never lasts, but if you win all the time, you are either cheating or playing with inferior opponents.

Seldom does the average person experience an incident where he/she can show real courage. Few of us will ever go to war, face down a bad guy, or complete our climb up the mountain despite the snowstorm. Most of us run into more mundane incidences, not seeing them as opportunities for manifesting courage. But every time we try anything, it takes at least a little courage. If we don't try—which means if we don't dare lose—courage is unnecessary, and *ipso facto*, success is unattainable. We then end up living off other people's major and minor courageous efforts.

As previously noted, people generally prefer success to failure. This is an unassailable premise that falls under the category of human nature, i.e. "common normality". Even people that prefer not trying, so they will not have to win, can hold a hidden pride about their success at being failures. Or they try to become good at being bad in order to be successful at drawing sympathy.

Success is not automatic and it may take a lot of effort to attain a goal. It is, after all, easier to do as little as possible, take advantage of what others have accomplished, and just get by. It takes courage to legitimately succeed at a goal because working toward success implies the possibility of wasting, at the very least, all the sweat, capital, and time that your effort required.

It especially takes courage to lose when you know that a fellow competitor has used unfair means to best you, but if you give up the *attempt* to win, you cannot possibly succeed, nor can you learn anything from the effort. If you know for sure that the cards are marked and stacked against you, you can, of course, wait for the next honest contest. Alternately, however, if you are *assuming* the cards are marked (i.e., if you are reframing negatively) in order to excuse yourself in case you lose…well, once again, don't bother entering. You probably won't win with that attitude, anyway.

Nike says, "Just Do it!" Tony Robbins tells us that no attitude can help one succeed without taking action. And Mel Robbins (no relationship to the above Tony) says to forget about the pep talks and self-motivation. She suggests that once you think of something on which you want to act, give yourself a five-second countdown, then spring into action—no excuses, no delays.

THE ACADEMY

Working as an instructor at Sumner "Mike" Burg's Academy of Physical and Social Development, a gymnasium school that helped kids (and some adults) with self-development through activity in various sports, I was required to write a brief report on every student for each class I had taught. The instructors' reports were very terse: checked boxes for the physical activities in which we participated and then a brief evaluation on how Johnny, Susie, or Sollie did, including any social or psychological characteristics we had noticed. One characteristic we frequently observed was "Fear of Failure". We would see a kid give a lackadaisical effort in floor hockey, pretending to be bored so that, if he were to fumble a pass or miss a shot, he could say, as an excuse, that he didn't really like floor hockey. The instructors worked hard not only to improve the kids' skills, but also to help them experience success in handling the pass or taking the shot. We found that just a little success would make them want to try harder. We also found that we needed to gloss over the kids' failures as "part of the game" so that Johnny, Susie, and Sollie could learn to gloss over those failures themselves, when no instructor was around.

The kids didn't know who Babe Ruth was. If they did, they might have realized that he not only led the league in home runs, but also in strikeouts. A more contemporary example of the same concept is Michael Jordan. My favorite Michael Jordan quote is, "I've missed more than 9000 shots in my career. I've lost almost 300 games. Twenty-six times I have been trusted to take the game winning shot and missed. I've failed over and over and over again in my life. And that's why I succeed." **Ignoring failure and emphasizing success is fundamental to a winning attitude.**

At The Academy, instead of having the "Just Do It" attitude, the "fear of failure" kid weighed his chances of success. Usually, his negativity was realistic when assessed with a broad perspective. The instructors tried to change that perspective. An instructor would attempt to reframe a boy's poor pass in floor hockey, for example, as a "tricky pass", one that had been essential to the instructor's scoring a goal. That made the kid successful in a scoring assist! That small step meant that Sollie would at least *attempt* the next pass. After a while, and after some training, the instructor might whisper to Sollie to station himself near the goal. Drawing the goalie out to one side, the instructor would pass to Sollie who had only to tip the puck in. Victory! Sollie scored his first floor hockey goal because the instructor had gotten him to gradually try a little more.

But what if Sollie had botched the simple shot? Wouldn't he feel even worse about himself? Maybe, but that could not erase his previous successes. The instructor would ignore the botch and try another tactic to give Sollie another small success, adding to that side of the ledger. This method is like NLP's tactic of mentally making negative images seem small and far away while making positive images seem close and large.

People tend to concentrate on what is immediate, so our attitude at The Academy was "let's make our students' success something upon which they are more likely to concentrate"—something recent (close) and important (relatively large).

The frequently asked question in self-development programs is, "What would you attempt to do if you knew you couldn't fail?" At The Academy we started with, "What would you attempt to do if you knew that you had a moderate chance of succeeding?" By small increments, we got the kids to try. That imbued the child with just an iota of courage—an iota more than he had had before. Daring to try meant daring to fail. Daring to fail meant losing occasionally, but it also meant getting more wins than any new kid who had a "fear of failure".

LOVE LOST

Without going too much into my personal life, I'll admit that, over the period of several decades, I felt so deeply about three women that losing them "broke my heart". The most recent was the worst because she was the best (that is, the best fit for me). We were a couple for almost five years, and it took me 2.5 years to get my head above water enough to be in psychological shape to try again.

You'd think, since this had happened two previous times, that I would know how to overcome the feeling of loss, and I actually did—intellectually. I could tell you what actions I should take and what attitudes I should assume. I knew the ropes. Emotionally, it was another matter. There was no possibility of my applying the efforts of my pre-fontal lobe (my logic) to this event. Sure, I'd try, but the amygdala (the older, reactionary part of the brain) dominated, no matter what clever techniques I used.

If I had been emotionally scarred two previous times, why did I bother going for number three? As the Dionne Warwick/Burt Bacharach song goes, "What do you get when you fall in love? / You only get lies and pain and sorrow. / So for at least until tomorrow, / I'll never fall in love again." Clearly, Dionne is telling us that although she was hurt, the desire to fall in love will win out in the end. Is it just part of human psychology to keep on keeping on in the face of such emotional pain, as Dionne suggests? Some of us decide that we weren't cut out for a relationship with a romantic partner and concentrate on writing poetry in our little Amherst, Massachusetts home. In contemporary society (circa 2019), some women have committed to radical feminism, feeling that "a woman needs a man like a fish needs a bicycle" (credit Gloria Steinem for that quote), while many men have joined the MGTOW (Men Going Their Own Way) Movement, avoiding romantic interaction with the opposite sex because it has simply become too complicated.

So, why did I decide, and continue to decide, to not give up on romance, knowing that the odds were against me? I certainly do not want to be presumptuous about the chances of finding a loving mate. Having dated for more decades than most people have lived, I can tell you that it does not get easier. Mature people know both what they want and what they are not willing to put up with. Experienced people know about "game" and have been given several reasons (in the form of untrustworthy partners) not to trust a new love interest. And yet, "no pain, no gain" is obviously the dominant sentiment when it comes to finding one's one-and-only.

Not to try is like committing emotional suicide. Perhaps you need courage to commit suicide, but you may need even more courage to keep on living. You may need courage to swear off the romantic scene, but you may need more courage to stay in that scene.

My "losing at love" did not last the first two times and I am planning for it to not to last again. After every painful break-up, I tried to learn as much as I could about (1) how I might have contributed to the demise of the relationship, (2) how the opposite sex thinks in ways I do not readily understand, and (3) what skills I can develop to make the next relationship work better.

Finding just *any* companion is not a problem. The challenge is to find a mutually loving companion that is also willing to soul-search and adjust to make her next relationship better than the last. If I settled for *any* relationship that might be in the offing, I would be doing myself (and my companion) a disservice. In order to win the relationship I want and that we both deserve (which means syncing on several levels), I have to take the chance that the relationship will not work (i.e., that at least one of those significant levels will not sync). In other words, in order to win at a high level, I have to risk losing in the process.

SUCCESSFUL BUSINESS vs. BUSINESS SUCCESS

When I was a martial arts teacher with only twenty years' experience, I was frustrated that teachers with half my experience were more successful at drawing in students than I. You would think that my being good at my art and being even better at teaching it would automatically draw in prospects. Such is not the case. Drawing in students has little or nothing to do with skills at teaching or knowledge of the subject being taught.

Recognizing this dichotomy, various martial arts business programs sprung up in the final quarter of the twentieth century—programs that would teach a guy like me to maximize a school's income. On the surface, that made perfect sense. The teacher/owner would be good at both the art and the teaching while the professional funding organization, to which the teacher paid a percentage of income, would be good at the business.

Unfortunately, the teacher, now thrilled with his increased financial success, tends to put his/her mind progressively more on maintaining or increasing the important revenue aspect of the business. As a martial arts factory, the school does well. In fact, it might even be a *good* factory that produces respectable products (its students). But in concentrating on the income of the business, there is a strong chance that the owner will put less emphasis on what *the students* may need to achieve a sense of success. The owner begins to measure the school's success not just in income, but in numbers of students, numbers of students promoted to black belt, and even the *reported* satisfaction of the student. If the student says she is happy with her initial goal of achieving a black belt, achieves it in the requisite 2.5 years, and becomes the 97th student to have done so, the owner considers the school a success. Achieving Black Belt is what students want, isn't it? By a strange circumnavigation, because the instructor feels his school is a success, the student feels that she is a success, as well. Because the student feels she is a success, the instructor considers his school a success.

I can tell you, having visited many such schools, that their students seldom have the consistent skills and depth of knowledge that the students of less financially successful, but more instruction-oriented, schools possess. One could argue that jealousy at a school's business success could bias my evaluation; however, I have sought the opinions of other instructors whose knowledge and skill I admire and most agree with me. Two other instructors, who did not agree, both admit that their junior students may not be as skilled as those of other instructors, but they claim that when those students reach upper black belt levels, they are at least as skilled as black belt students of other schools. There are several factors in this debate that are not relevant to this discussion, but what seems to be agreed upon is that Sensei Fred McFunding has won the contest with Sensei Tom McTeach. He hasn't cheated, but he has unconsciously changed the standards by which schools were once measured. How frustrating that must be for Sensei McTeach! McTeach hasn't failed exactly, but he has not succeeded in bringing that average black-belt-seeking student into his dojo because, in *his* school, it takes 4-5 years to earn that rank, and to the new student, that seems too long a commitment.

Consider me in the McTeach category. Many times I wondered why I kept on keeping on with a low annual income and fewer students to go out into the world and spread the word. I did not want to sacrifice quality for a greater quantity of dollars and I was committed to providing interested students with a source of substantive, high-level, traditional martial arts. To give up on that goal would mean that the martial arts world would be a little less well-informed, and a little more willing to settle for mediocrity. Although I felt I was competing with martial arts instructors that did not know the details of their arts as well as I, those same instructors were decidedly superior at knowing the market. It would be a challenge for me to keep going, but to cash in while maintaining a school that even a lower-ranked student could maintain would have left me both unchallenged and unsatisfied.

I dared to run a different route, taking the chance that I might not succeed and even lose financially. Did I win ultimately? Not if dollars in the bank are the measurement of victory, but my scores of educational videos and books, according to many who have learned from them, have advanced the martial artists in ways they might not have been advanced if I had opted only for monetary success.

THE EASY WAY OUT

As I noted in the sections on Truth, some people manipulate as much as possible, cheating in order to win while pretending that their cheating was just playing "hard ball".

In the early months of my teaching at The Academy of Physical and Social Development, I thought that their reframing success for kids, their instructors' conspiring to allow a child to succeed "artificially", and their penchant for measuring success relatively rather than absolutely, was the equivalent of cheating. In my estimation at the time, it was cheating for a good cause, but it was still cheating.

I was wrong. The strategy of The Academy was not to deceive in order to win at someone else's expense, not even to give artificial success to kids so that parents would keep paying for lessons—that would be taking the easy way out. Rather, The Academy's strategy was to have the kids play in contests in which they *could*, in fact, succeed, where no contests like these existed in the larger culture. Their measurement of success was relative in the way a high school basketball player's success is relative to success at playing for the Celtics. Different levels of play imply different standards. The Academy was employing a simple—and supremely rational—approach to teaching: start with simple block letter printing and stay with those letters until the student is ready for cursive writing.

The Academy was not cheating, nor playing "hard ball", and it was certainly not taking the easy way out. By showing the student that his losses amounted to no more than stepping stones first to small, and then to larger victories, The Academy was gradually inspiring the student to reframe his own life so that he could eventually live in the reality of that reframe.

AS APPLIED TO LIFE

Love and business are two of the biggest aspects of one's wider life. As such, they set the stage for one's attitude about persistence. Tony Robbins suggests (while admittedly reframing the way most people think about attaining a desired result) that everyone's efforts *always* get a result. In that sense, we always succeed. The trick to arriving at a *desired* result is to either parlay or adjust your attained result again and again, like a gymnast constantly adjusts his balance in a handstand, or a pilot constantly adjusts her course. That means that in the process of succeeding, you are losing your balance or veering off course most of the time until you arrive at your goal!

Be aware, however, that once having arrived, once having succeeded, there is more to achieve, and that means renewing one's courage to dare. Renewing one's courage to dare means once again facing the potential of failure or loss.

Repeating one's attempts when the chances are high that one will not succeed may be worth the effort because success **accumulates and losses do not (unless you let them)**! In his book *Principles*, Ray Dalio writes: "…while one gets better at things over time, it doesn't become any easier if one is also progressing to higher levels—the Olympic athlete finds his sport to be every bit as challenging as the novice does." And then later: "If you're not failing, you're not pushing your limits, and if you're not pushing your limits, you're not maximizing your potential."

Dare to lose in love, in business, and in life—losing never lasts but if you win all the time, you are either cheating or playing with inferior opponents.

5.

COURAGE:

"What could have been" can be painful and debilitating—realize the simple fact that it could not have been.

When we plan for success, we naturally "future-pace", that is, we imagine what life will be like when we achieve our goal. Losses in any area of life seem to stimulate the part of the psyche that "reminisces" about those things that did not happen, but in our fantasies, could have. I imagined that I would retire, with the love of my life, to a state warmer than the New England states, and enjoy developing a retirement business with her while discovering new restaurants and planning new travels.

Of course, you can't literally *reminisce* about the future, can you? Feeling sentimental about what could have been is future-pacing the benefits of achieving a goal when you should either abandon or at least adjust that goal. Thinking about "what could have been" is like spending an investment's return despite the fact that the investment has tanked.

After a loss, it is not unusual to wallow in sorrow for some amount of time. I have found that the more intense the emotional commitment to the goal, the more time it takes to admit that the goal has to be reset. For example, I found that for the three romantic break-ups that I experienced, it took precisely 50% of the duration of the relationship to over-come the what-could-have-been sorrows. If the relationship lasted two years, it took me one year to accept its loss. If it lasted five years, it took another 2.5 years to actually move on. However, if the last two of those five years were trouble-some and less intense than the first three, it would take a shorter time to adjust, since the adjustments would have been happening concurrent with the relationship. Therefore, little if any melancholy or sentimentality would infect the wound. In fact, the wound would hardly have a scar. Conversely, if the break-up was sudden, shocking, and without any chance of reconciliation, the 50% rule consistently applied.

What could possibly diminish this long-term pain—pain that is often accompanied by a debilitating depression? Answer: consciously realizing that there is no such thing as "what could have been". "What could have been" is just our imagination holding onto that which we valued even though it is no longer with us. "What could have been" is looking at the rear view mirror and pretending it is the windshield.

BUILD YOU UP JUST TO LET YOU DOWN

In the early years of this millennium, I was in pretty good financial shape. My father had left me a duplex that was providing rental income and I was also renting out the condominium apartment from which I had moved in the mid-1990s. I was living in my big, new condo with a girl-friend who was happy to pay a modest share of our expenses because it cost her much less than living alone, and I had discovered a private investment that was earning a great deal of passive income.

I made small contributions to this investment at first, making sure to draw cash out from time to time to check the reliability of the fund. Due diligence having been done, I saw the account grow at a rapid rate. That had me future-pacing how, in just two or three more months, I would be able to apportion the money. I would be frugal until the amount in the fund hit a million dollars, after which time I would draw out a portion of each month's dividends while maintaining a reasonably large principle to earn income. After having saved and planned for years, I would finally be able to afford a much more expensive car and to travel with my girlfriend whenever we desired. I even wrote how much I would withdraw each year to live on and how much I would donate to three or four of my favorite charities.

First, my girlfriend seemed to lose interest in me—I suspect she was seeing several other people, but I can't be sure because she would not talk about our relationship or how to improve it. Eventually, she moved out. The loss of a partner is painful, but these things happen, and because the relationship had been dwindling on the vine, I could say, "Okay, good luck!"

Then, a tenant defaulted on his rent and another tenant with a new child discovered that there was lead-based paint in one of my father's rental apartments. The de-leading would cost me $50,000. I won't go into the expenses and annoyance dealing with the two properties. I drew out funds to pay for the refurbishing. Once through all of this, I sold my father's duplex so I could invest more into the large, profitable fund. A short while later, just before I reached my million-dollar goal, I saw my main investment evaporate because of a well orchestrated and difficult-to-detect fraud. On paper, I lost $890,000 in the main investment, and during the same period, lost another $20,000 in a separate investment.

I found myself approaching retirement alone, and with only few thousand dollars remaining in several other accounts. Ironically, I was not crazed, sad, or even angry—at least not for long. I had seen the loss of my girlfriend coming a mile off, and once it was clear that she was unwilling to remedy the situation, I knew we would be better apart than together. I handled the monetary loss with an aplomb that even surprised me, probably because I had grown up in a low-income family in which there were few frills. I had gone to an expensive university, but I had been fortunate to secure both a scholarship and a government loan to do so. Even though I had not been making a lot of money at the time, I had paid back the loan conscientiously only a few years after graduation. I knowingly had opted to work in a field that would not make me rich, so I had developed the habit of being frugal. Having lived without a lot of things all my life, I knew living that way again would be annoying, but not impossible.

I spent almost no time at all on the "what-could-have-beens". Sure, there were times that I was frustrated because I could not take the vacations that I had been able to take when I was earning more money, and I did have to deal with a low-level of depression from time to time, wondering just how I could pull myself up and return to the independent me I wanted to be. Reality was going to demand that I do things I would not normally have opted to do, but perhaps I could find a way to climb out of the pit of necessity and bask occasionally on the beach of independence.

These circumstances were very unusual. I had succeeded in going from a mere "thousandaire" to a millionaire in less than a decade! Just as unusual were the succession of loses. Seldom do two tenants, one girlfriend, and two investments crash in the same field—and all within a few years. Without verbalizing the concept aloud, I recognized that "what could have been" might have happened in fantasy if the world were different, but in this reality, the world was what it was, so "what could have been" simply could not have been.

It's human nature to pine over what we thought we had or could have had, even to the point of torturing ourselves with images of things that really could not have been. **We do not control reality. We control only our preparations for eventualities and our responses to actualities.**

Ironically, when something we want to happen actually *does* occur, we don't spend any time thinking about the losses that could have happened. If we win the lottery, we don't waste a second thinking, "Gosh, if only I had played this number last week, I would have lost!" Those people that often and regularly fantasize about what could go wrong are called neurotic.

Similarly, if something minor we'd *like* to happen *doesn't* occur, we waste little time thinking about what could have been. We either forget about it or get to work doing something about it. Most of us don't bother ourselves with things that could go wrong beyond the normal, everyday caution and care. If it is broken, we repair it, or throw it out and try again.

Tony Robbins tells us that people are more motivated by the potential of loss than the potential of gain. We work harder to *keep* something than we work to *gain* something. If we dare to be scrupulously honest (Principle #2) even if it means losing, if we dare to fail momentarily (Principle #3, *Don't represent a reframe as objective truth*), knowing that a failure can make us better people (as we discussed in Principle # 4, *Dare to lose in love, in business, and in life...*), inevitably we will have to face the cold fact of losing a love, a substantial amount of money, or an important opportunity. Loss is always painful, but that pain does not have to last.

Being truthful with yourself means that you accept reality as it is. No, you don't accept it as a permanent state, but as a transitory occurrence because you are part of that reality and have an influence on it. **It is an expression of courage to face reality without fantasy, without unearned guilt, and with as little remorse as possible.**

"What could have been" can be painful and debilitating—realize the simple fact that it could not have been.

Re: COURAGE

"Success is not final, failure is not fatal: it is the courage to continue that counts." — attributed to Winston S. Churchill

"It takes courage to grow up and become who you really are." — e. e. cummings

"I wanted you to see what real courage is, instead of getting the idea that courage is a man with a gun in his hand. It's when you know you're licked before you begin, but you begin anyway and see it through no matter what. [-- Atticus Finch]" — Harper Lee, *To Kill a Mockingbird*

"The most courageous act is still to think for yourself. Aloud." — Coco Chanel

6.

INDEPENDENCE:

Support or contribute to any cause you can validate, not one that simply sounds good—an un-validated cause may represent the opposite of what you value. Refrain, however, from membership in movements, parties, or protests. Not only do their beliefs and means tend to change over time, but your joining may make you feel obligated to defend what they stand for, rather than think for yourself.

I am sure that readers who feel a need for community will balk at the middle sentence of this principle (Refrain…from memberships…). So many people feel that without a membership in something, they are doomed to live as hermits in the center of a dark forest on the outskirts of Meaninglessville. Remember, however, that the principle urges you to "refrain" rather than "revoke" or "reject". Rather than abjuring common causes when appropriate, I am more advocating for understanding the implications of membership in a movement, party, or cause.

The old saying goes: "If you don't stand for something, you'll fall for anything." Unfortunately, in today's messy world, the thing you stand for may be the very thing you have fallen for.

I have often described a certain woman with whom I went to college (I'll call her Jewel) this way: "She never met a protest she didn't like." Jewel not only marched for Civil Rights and against The Vietnam War in the '60s, she continued her participation even after she had retired in her 60s. That she was an activist did not surprise me, given her politics. What did surprise me was her adherence to whatever the wing of her party expected of her, as if she had gotten both the talking points and the marching orders from central command each morning.

If we were to discuss an issue (here I'll choose something both fictitious and innocuous), she would make a passionate argument against women wasting money on gaudy bracelets, earrings, and necklaces when there are poor unfortunates who cannot afford even a simple metal wristband. She would say that owning bracelets, earrings, and necklaces just make rich jewelers richer while simultaneously making the poor feel sorry for themselves. I never could understand how, on a protest march in Boston, Jewel could not see the irony in her organization's buying thousands of engraved metal wristbands to flaunt as symbols during her march, while never giving any of her own real jewelry or urging others to give their jewelry to the poor. I would have pointed out that the thousands of those metal wristbands worn at the protest were bought from a fairly well off Boston jeweler, but I doubt if she would be willing to see the irony.

TOGETHER AND ALONE

I grew up feeling, as I assume most kids did, that whatever my family did was standard operating procedure for most other families. Then, having realized that not every family did what we did, I assumed that my family *must* be a cut above normal. I said to myself that obviously we had made good choices; after all, some families were struggling financially more than we were, or were in crisis with their kids. As a child, it seemed apparent to me that although things could get better, they also could have been a lot worse, so in the future, making choices like my family had made was the reasonable way to go. Of course, what passed for "choices" when I was a little kid concerned everyday aspects of life like the brands we bought at the supermarket, the TV shows we watched, or how often we chose to visit relatives, as if those mundane items could magically affect the success of a family unit. I think my idea that "choices" were important was pretty astute for a youngster, yet my experience about what constituted important choices was non-existent.

As I matured and was faced with my own decisions, minor as they might have been for a young boy, I began to notice that my mom and dad differed in their personal choices. Each favored a different brand of cigarette, each took their post-prandial coffee differently, and one of them (my mom) was better at math, while the other (my dad) was better at drawing. In other words, although we were a family group, we were also independent individuals.

Noted I to myself: we are individuals in a collective. As a child, that collective was not of my choosing, of course. I could not choose to be with another family or to live alone, so I accepted the group I was in, honored it, but did not always concur with its selections. Having thought the commonplace choices we had made were magical, I now decided that there was more magic in being an individual. For example, although both my parents smoked, I decided never to smoke. Back then, we weren't fully knowledgeable about the health risks of smoking, but I knew that I didn't like the smell, the taste, the squinty eyes, or my dad's coughing every morning.

My father stopped going to church because he often had to work on Sundays. To compensate, he refrained from eating meat on Wednesdays in addition to observing the normal Friday restrictions that most Catholics recognized. After a while, my mother also decided not to go to church on Sunday, but I was expected both to attend Mass and also to attend Confraternity of Christian Doctrine (CCD) classes on Thursday evenings. Yep, my Sunday school was on Thursdays. And, being a good kid, who wanted to do right by my parents (and be on God's good side), I set aside those times so that my attendance would be perfect. A good student, I learned all sorts of things about my given faith that my parents did not know. I even worked at the church's rectory (where the priests lived) every other evening during high school.

I missed attending church only once because I was sick. But I did miss numerous Thursday evening classes because, while working at the rectory, the priests gave me a special dispensation from CCD on Thursday nights so I could attend their phone, their door, and sell Mass cards to aggrieved parishioners. I guess they couldn't see paying me ($1 per hour back then) for going to my CCD class rather than doing my job.

Later, I would describe those days as my super-Catholic period. More than one reverent adult asked me if I were considering the priesthood. OMG! Absolutely not! I knew even back then that (1) I liked girls too much to become celibate forever, and (2) I did not want the regional bishop, or even the Pope telling me what to think or how to act. Ironic, isn't it? I was an obedient child for the most part, and an observant Catholic, but I had a really strong independent streak.

Throughout my time attending CCD classes, I often asked questions that the brothers and the lay teachers did not answer to my satisfaction. But they were the authorities, so I had to accept their responses as the best answers the religion could offer me at my present stage of development...or theirs.

I tried to square my religious beliefs (rather, Catholicism's beliefs) with what I knew about life, human nature, misbehavior and crime, the church, science, and esoteric things like alternate views of the universe and the potential of an afterlife. To be frank, after several years of being a cafeteria Catholic (choosing what beliefs and practices made sense to me), I had to admit that I was not representing The Catholic Gentleman well nor being honest with myself. If I were to continue in the Catholic "club" I would have had to make excuses for either parts of the faith or parts of the Catholic hierarchy with which I simply did not agree.

I asked myself in this early philosophical phase, at what point is a member of a group no longer a valid member? Most people just continue on their own, ignoring the tenets of their "group", and never acknowledge having left their affiliations behind—i.e., Catholics say they are Catholics even though they no longer go to church; Democrats say they are democrats even though they personally prefer lower taxes and fewer regulations; Republicans still claim to be Republicans even though they look forward to collecting Social Security. Because they are loath to relinquish their memberships, these MINOs (Members in Name Only) serve neither their "team" nor another "team", but are tripping towards being a team unto themselves. They dislike that option, too, because it would leave them unsupported and un-companioned. Often they avoid abandoning team membership because it would leave them without an identity. And so they claim membership in a group, and support it with their actions, albeit not with their beliefs.

As a child, I played "war" with friends in the park behind my house. I am not sure if this was inspired by the 1950s movies or the fact that our fathers had fought in World War II. No one ever played the enemy—he was always imaginary. Therefore, we never had to "shoot" at each other or feign a death. Sure, once in a while someone took an imaginary bullet burn in the leg or arm, but by and large, we enjoyed jumping behind rocks and bushes, being the heroes without a physical foe. In those days, the enemy had been obvious: a Nazi was a bad dude who was not only eager to shoot us, but eager to take over the country in some sort of totalitarian regime that we were too young to imagine. In my neighborhood, no one was Jewish, so the fight never took on a more ominous meaning.

During elementary school, I wrestled in my backyard. During junior high and high school, I played football. I was certainly used to rough and tumble. But I did not get into actual fights because, as a good Catholic boy, I did not want to be in a position to have to hurt someone. One time, Big Jim C. had one of his lieutenants request my presence in the State Park's bathhouse and slugged me for spending five minutes talking to the girl in whom he was interested.

Several peers who witnessed this were shocked that I neither panicked nor fought back. To do either seemed rather stupid to me. Panic would not have helped my self-respect or the audience's respect for me. Fighting would be futile since not only was Jim larger than I, not only was his father a former prizefighter, but also he had cronies in the audience where I had several witnesses but no allies. Either my refusal to fight was being wise or cowardly. Luckily, Big Jim relented.

After high school, the federal government made the decision to almost, but not quite, conduct a war in Vietnam. In college, I was old enough to understand that LBJ did not want to lose, but was not exactly eager to have our military pull out all the stops, either. He was holding back, and he had not even been a good Catholic boy!

So there I was, soon to graduate college and face the draft, not being able to fully identify with my war games youth and yet not eager to fight a war where the military, in my humble opinion, was not allowed to fully engage. To be frank, if they had fully engaged, I don't know if my super-Catholic self would have been ready to join them. I was, in essence facing another Big Jim.

On top of the government's mismanagement of the war, I had to deal with the threat of conscription, which I felt was both un-American and ineffective. Many drafted soldiers did not want to be there, spent their time in-country getting stoned, and simply did not have the fighting spirit that our fathers proudly displayed during WWII. The stateside resistance to the war seemed to be principled, but those principles came in from every angle and were inconsistent at best. There were the moral resistors who felt killing anyone for any reason, war or no war, was evil. There were the economic resisters who claimed that the USA wanted to conquer Vietnam for its natural resources. The eco-resisters bled (excuse the term) into the political resistors, who claimed that conquest was an inevitable result of capitalism's drive toward economic expansion and the West's drive toward colonialism. Not only did I recognize the other side of each of these arguments, but also I recognized that the arguments were being made by hippies who did more dope than the soldiers in 'Nam. At the ages of 18 through 22, the protestors claimed to somehow know international politics and warfare better than professional politicians and military men, and believed that constant rallies and civil unrest (often a pseud-onym for public violence in mobs) was the way to show their displeasure with official policy.

I was like the blind man touching the elephant of truth. Every aspect I touched seemed part of a larger whole, the entirety of which I could not grasp. I did not want to be a part of any of these "groups"; rather, I wanted to be left alone. I disrespected both the government's conduct of the war and the resistor's conduct of the resistance.

After two years of soul-searching and misery, I had the good fortune to escape military service via the draft lot-tery. The final number drawn that year was 95. Mine was 99. Saved from having to make a life-and-death decision, I was free to reflect on my beliefs and which "team" I was really on. I found that I could be sure only of the teams I was not on. I was too young and ignorant to validate the "causes" before me. Both sides, it seemed, counted heavily on their ability to mislead. What the government claimed it was doing might not have been what it was really doing. What the protestors claimed they believed in might not have been what they really believed in.

Just before President Nixon pulled the United States out of Vietnam, I decided to attend one of the Marches on Washington that protested the war. I generally did not like marches, feeling that protests served to unify one side and simultaneously stiffen the opposite side, but since I had never taken time from my studies to be a Freedom Rider or march with Dr. King during the civil rights era, I felt that I should act to somehow show my distaste for the war. Now that I was safe from being drafted, no one could argue that my marching was simply because I wanted the war to stop before I was forced to fight. I drove down to DC with my British girlfriend, stayed overnight in a nice home owned by relatives of friends, visited The Smithsonian, and the next day assembled with a thousand other marchers. They soon became eight to ten thousand.

How we managed to convene is still a mystery to me. Someone on a bullhorn said we were moving to such and such an avenue and from there would walk down such and such a street. How would we get there? Did Mistress Bullhorn think that we carried street maps with us? Nevertheless, we marched. Songs broke out and they quickly morphed into chants. Groups of people had brought banners and signs. I don't remember any suggestion that we arrive thus prepared, but there we were, marching along the margin of a street-wide column that was chanting, "Powwwer to the People. Hey, Hey!" Wait a minute! That sounded suspiciously like a Communist sentiment to me—not something for which we had signed up.

Halfway though the march, I saw some young men in an adjoining street attempting to overturn a car. Had the automobile threatened to kill innocent Vietnamese? Had the automobile been complicit in drafting young adults before they could attend grad school? This demonstration was making no sense to me. And then I realized that its nonsense, its chaos, its violence was making sense in a wider sense. Many of us marchers were being co-opted into representing causes in which we did not necessarily believe. The protest, in which I had planned to participate, had morphed into one I would never have joined, and now my girlfriend and I were lending our bodies to causes that could not have convinced us with a rational argument, but had been skilled at taking advantage of our anti-Vietnam emotions.

When I indicate that I am not a "joiner", people understandably point out that I was a member of many sports teams, serving as captain of my high school gymnastics team and my college flag football team, that I was the head of martial arts system, a federation, and that I currently operate a martial arts school. Certainly these were "groups" with "causes", weren't they? Yes, but they were groups and causes that I could easily validate. There was no deception in the idea that Ashland High School's football team wanted to beat Hopkinton High School's football team. That's why we were there. There was no surreptitious changing of plans when my federation or dojo activated its "policy" to both teach and recognize rank in a specific family of martial arts. We did not change martial arts or our *raison d'etre* when no one was looking. And most importantly, we did not guilt members into espousing a point of view. Want to play for our team? Join. Not interested? Fine—live long and prosper.

Teams and other groups, political or otherwise, exist because people are both individualistic and gregarious. Unless human nature takes an unfortunate turn toward solitude, people will continue to join groups. Solitude, after all, would result in fewer human beings to continue the species. Because both partnership and community is so important to people, it follows that the choice of the community with which one associates should be careful and well informed—at least as careful and well informed as the choice of a partner.

People join a group for a selfish reason, not necessarily to enrich themselves directly, but to accomplish something they want to accomplish, but could not as easily have done alone. Some people join a group to have more fun than they could have solo, or to contribute to a cause in a larger way than writing a check. Other people join groups because it is too difficult to walk one's own individual path, or because one feels incapable of standing out, or because one feels unsure which ideas to support and which to oppose. Some people join groups to feel life swirling around them while they retire to a quiet corner, not totally alone, but not involved enough to join the dance. In other words, some people have thought about what they can accomplish by joining a group, others want the group to think for them and even to determine their actions. How often do you see a friend post a political party's talking points on social media, as if those clever phrases had been visited upon him in a personal revelation that he has now generously chosen to share with the ignorant masses? You see it every other post. Conversely, how many people refuse to post anything until they have sorted through several points of view and have decide what they truly believe? Few, if any.

Although I have participated in many groups, I clearly favor a concentration on developing one's own well-researched, well-thought-out point of view. Why? Because from these clearly delineated, defendable personal points of view are philosophies formed. Around those philosophies, groups and causes assemble. If I were to join a group or favor a cause, it would not be because its statements "feel" right, nor because I have allowed the collective to think for me, but because that group or cause articulates my philosophy more accurately or fully than I.

When a group governs a member, it is only logical that members will voluntarily relinquish some of their individual ideas so that the group can work in unison. When a group becomes the dominant origin of thought, however, you can be sure that select *individuals* (or in some cases, one dominant individual) in those groups are not relinquishing *their* ideas, but establishing the group's positions behind the scenes. Those individuals want to gain strength in numbers by making *their* thoughts *the group's* thoughts. Groupthink starts with individuals who do not want to stand alone, thus conspire to bring other less clear-thinking people into the fold.

EARLY GROUPTHINK

While in college, I stopped by a convenience store to buy razors. A guy about my age leaned toward me and said, "You don't want to buy Schick."

I figured he knew something about some flaw in production I hadn't heard about. "Why not?" I asked.

"They support the war," was his response.

I immediately reached for the Gillette shavers. Then I became curious and a little angry. I had no way to know if Schick supported the war or not. Nor did I know if Bic or Gillette had taken some political position. Also, I was not in the habit of boycotting a company for any reason, let alone a reason that could not be verified. Why then, did I reach for another brand even after my unknown informant had departed? I suspect that I was responding emotionally and unconsciously yielding to groupthink. That stranger was my age and was probably facing the draft as I was. But what else did we have in common? And why would commonalities matter anyway? He had assumed that since we were alike in one way, we would be alike in other ways. It was a late 1960s version of identity politics. I was supposed to identify with a group and thus conform to its preferred actions. There was no Internet, no cell phone service, no email, or other way to connect with "like minded" fellows, so the old word-of-mouth method did the trick, instead. I did not realize it then, but his very assumption that I would conform made me instantaneously want to conform since I was clearly part of his group—same age group, same dislike for the war. As fate would have it, my preference for independent thinking gave me enough pause to consider both my situation and how conformity would be spread among the non-conformists of the day. Frozen in the headlights of uncertainty, I bought a single Schick out of stubbornness and vowed to learn more about what had happened.

PERSONAL RESPONSIBILITY

People too often make decisions based not on facts and research, but on impressions. Tony Robbins came up with a calculus that pretty consistently can predict the outcome of most political races. He asks, "Which candidate is more physically attractive? Which candidate is more inspiring? Which candidate's positions are more consistent?" Think about that for a moment. Do any of those three qualities have anything to do with facts or logic? Rather, they are concerned with providing the voter with a positive impression. I would submit that general impressions are the dominant influence for most voters, not which political point of view has been historically validated, not which point of view relates to reality (i.e. tells the truth), not which point of view, if put into action, would likely function as predicted after the election.

Every election season, media personalities urge citizens to vote! Why? Obviously, it is because they do not want their preferred candidate to lose because of lack of turnout, but that's not what they say. They tell you that voting is our sacred duty as free people. That always sits wrong with me. The more duty I have, the less I feel free. I would argue that more people should stay home. That is not our duty, but it is our right. Since the majority of potential voters do not vote on the majority of issues but on their favorite single issue or on their general impression of a candidate, how does their vote help elect the more qualified candidate?

Single-issue voters think they know the details of that issue, but then, because of that one issue, they align with a party whose other issues they do not fully understand and with which they might not agree, were they to understand them. Because that party claims to support their single issue, the voter gets the *impression* that that party is best for them. In other words, they go on a peaceful March on Washington to support one cause and are willing to ignore those in the group that are overturning cars in support of another.

My elderly aunt who had voted in more elections that I had years on the planet claimed that she would vote for Candidate P for governor. My cousins and I knew my aunt's personality and her stated beliefs. We believed that Candidate P stood for policies with which my aunt would not agree. Why, we asked, would she vote for Candidate P? "Well," she explained, "he grew up poor like me." My cousins and I were aghast! My aunt's single issue was not even a single issue! She would cast her vote for a candidate who would probably enact policies with which she would disagree, and she would do so only because (1) her past had something in common with that candidate's past, and (2) she felt obliged to vote regardless of her knowledge (or ignorance) of the election issues. If I reframe the incident, I can claim that she was at least "thinking for herself", thus avoiding any party line, but could her individual point of view be considered well-validated or even rational? More importantly, was it *responsible*?

Rand wrote: "America's founding ideal was the principle of individual rights. ... The rest was the logical consequence of fidelity to that one principle." Similarly, I believe that, for the most part, an ideal society grows from individual *responsibility*. The success of the society flows from the logical consequences that follow. I do not mean responsibility to others or to one's church, or any other duty that has not been consciously assumed. I mean responsibility to one's own wellbeing. In my humble opinion, you should take seriously the responsibility of deeply understanding any candidate you favor and any group you choose to join.

The less an individual *needs* a group to lend him aid, the healthier the society is. This is true whether you are for minimal government or for a welfare state. A minimal government supporter stays away from welfare or other social benefits therefore taking the chance that private charity will support those in dire straits. A welfare-statist feels that private charity will fail to help enough people so the government must compel others to pay for third-party help. In either case, if we start with the idea that people have the responsibility to take care of themselves in every area of their life and will be expected to do so, either a minimal government or a welfare state would be much easier to manage and/or afford.

In the same way, the less the individual depends on memberships in groups to substitute for her own individual reasoning, the less likely that individual's mind will be co-opted by a groupthink that may not be in her personal interest.

If you are charitable enough to feel an obligation to help others, you must decide who to help and with *how much* money, time, or effort. That is a decision based on personal responsibility. It would be irresponsible for you to promise help and then not be able to follow through. Whether you are on the Left or Right, personal responsibility should be your aspiration, your objective, and the lynchpin to your political policies. Further, if personal responsibility is not central to your policies when they are put into practice, i.e. if some other entity has to be responsible for things, you may be unwittingly advocating that the might of the government should enforce your personal view of society. Imagine if everyone thought that way. Do you really want that sort of autocracy? Who would win influence if everyone decided not to accept responsibility for his/her own little piece of the puzzle? Autocracy would likely turn into plutocracy (government by the wealthy), since the wealthy could most easily buy their way into power.

If the application of legal force is your unspoken answer, consider reevaluating your point of view or consider creating relatively painless incentives for people to become more personally responsible. Often governments or other organizations create artificial incentives that reward one kind of action and mildly punish another without the need for external force. This used to happen in society without having to invent artificial carrots or sticks. We used to call these incentives conventions. More on this in Principle #7, below.

Support or contribute to any cause you can validate, not one that simply sounds good—an un-validated cause may represent the opposite of what you value. Refrain, however, from membership in movements, parties, or protests. Not only do their beliefs and means tend to change over time, but your joining may make you feel obligated to defend what they stand for, rather than think for yourself.

Re: INDEPENDENCE

"I care for myself. The more solitary, the more friendless, the more unsustained I am, the more I will respect myself." — Charlotte Brontë, *Jane Eyre*

"To find yourself, think for yourself." — often attributed to Socrates

"If you truly want to be respected by people you love, you must prove to them that you can survive without them." — Michael Bassey Johnson, *The Infinity Sign*

"It is easier to live through someone else than to complete yourself. The freedom to lead and plan your own life is frightening if you have never faced it before. It is frightening when a woman finally realizes that there is no answer to the question 'who am I' except the voice inside herself." — Betty Friedan

"The proverb warns that, 'You should not bite the hand that feeds you.' But maybe you should, if it prevents you from feeding yourself." — Thomas Stephen Szasz

"We are so accustomed to the comforts of 'I cannot', 'I do not want to', and 'it is too difficult' that we forget to realize when we stop doing things for ourselves and expect others to dance around us, we are not achieving greatness. We have made ourselves weak." — Pandora Poikilos, *Excuse Me, My Brains Have Stepped Out*

7.

CONVENTIONS:

Conventions and customs are not unassailable, but without them there is chaos. Argue against them, if you wish, but in so doing, present an alternative that will work. If, over time, you find your alternative does not work, accept that the original convention, albeit flawed, has value. Neither NEW nor OLD is necessarily better. All things must prove their objective worth; otherwise, they are just personal preferences.

With all this talk about thinking for oneself, you'd think that I was a born iconoclast. *Au contraire, mon ami.* While I don't mind "clasting" down cultural icons now and then, I generally have a respect for tradition—*rational* tradition. That's why my sense of individualism finds no conflict with my being a *traditional* martial artist. The Asian martial arts are sometimes steeped in traditions that Westerners do not understand and thus consider no more than mere rigmarole; however, if they are not overdone, martial traditions serve valid purposes regarding both respect and safety. In other words, the traditions of the traditional martial arts are often quite rational.

In my book of everyday martial arts tales, *The Dojo Files*, I revisit a lesson about tradition that several other writers and speakers have presented.

There is an old story about a family gathering in which Momma is cooking a roast. She cuts off both ends of the roast before it goes into the oven. Her daughter asks why she does that. "That's how my mother taught me to cook a roast. I don't know why. Grandma is in the other room, though, so let's ask her." In response to the same question, Grandma says, "Why, I don't know. That's how my mother taught me. Great Grandma is taking a nap right now. When she wakes up, let's ask her." A few minutes later, Great Grandmother slowly takes her place at the dining room table beside her daughter, granddaughter, and great granddaughter. "Mother," inquires Grandma, "when you taught me to cook a roast, you always cut off the ends. Why do we do that?"

"Hmmm. Damn oven was too small."

Clearly, some traditions are followed blindly. Every new generation seems to feel accosted by the traditions they "must" follow and fancies itself as the generation that will finally break free of useless traditions that their progenitors have been too ignorant or weak-willed to challenge.

My generation, which came to young adulthood in the late 1960s, was as non-conformist a generation as one could imagine. Our parents had lived through The Great Depression, World War II, and the Korean conflict. They are called The Greatest Generation because of the courage and nobility they showed in facing all of that. My generation, however, did not settle for the relative prosperity and tranquility that our parents wanted for us.

Not having to buckle down to work for family survival, not being threatened by the idea of a Nazi or Nipponese takeover of the hemisphere, the children of The Greatest Generation, the young Baby Boomers, had to deal only with a *cold* war; however, it is important to note that that cold war held the constant threat of global nuclear annihilation. As they matured, The Boomers also had to deal with a series of turbulences that remind me of that old Chinese curse, "May you live in interesting times."

As my generation approached adulthood, Vietnam was beginning to overwhelm our attention. At the same time, The Civil Rights Movement, The Woman's Movement, the availability of soft and hard drugs, The Sexual Revolution, and the advent of birth control created unique cultural pressures with which no one had previous dealt. Existing conventions did not afford us a tried-and-true path around or through.

It was understandable, I think, that we challenged every convention that seemed to get in the way of dealing with all those new influences. In fact, convention itself seemed to be the enemy. After all, wasn't it convention that said you should not curse, that you should go to church on Sundays, save money for retirement, sacrifice for your children, and look down with pity upon other countries' governmental systems? Wasn't it convention that said you should not live with someone before you marry him or her? Wasn't it convention that kept women earning less than men? Weren't regional conventions keeping African-Americans under Jim Crow laws?

We simply did not perceive our society, our culture, or our country the same way our parents did. To complicate matters, although we were not half as tough as our parents, we were much better educated. At nineteen years old, for example, we were more knowledgeable and astute about the world than our parents had been; but we were also much less experienced. And because we had never had to make our way in the real world (let alone contribute to a larger family), we were *much less responsible*. And there we were, trying to make broad cultural changes simply because we weren't satisfied with the conventions we had inherited. How many people reading this book now would take political, career, or investment advice from a 19-year-old? How many could live their lives the way a 19-year-old wants to live hers?

Yet we 19-year-olds argued against conventions and wanted to remove them, even though we had no idea how they served society. Nor did we consider how we might replace them. For us, societal conventions were eminently assailable, but we could not envision the chaos that would ensue without them. We thought that we would be freer once they were gone. Isn't that why our parents fought against the Axis powers? Wasn't freedom the characteristic of society we most cared about? Weren't our parents being hypocritical if they did not support our desire for more and more freedom?

Religious and cultural conventions keep people moving in predictable and mutually acceptable ways without having to fashion laws to restrict them. Freedom becomes chaos if it is not directed and controlled in some way. Conversely, direction and control can turn into restriction and confinement when they come more from the outside than from within. **Convention and religion merely put pressure on individuals to control their own license; on the other hand, laws and governments forcibly restrict individuals from disobeying whatever the legislators consider proper behavior. The former elicit social pressure but do not contain the threat of force. The latter use threat of force to elicit social pressure.**

To us 19-year-old Baby Boomers, The Old seemed nonfunctional and hypocritical. The New, by contrast, seemed desirable even though we could not see where The New would lead. All of the above can be blamed on energetic, idealistic, or even rambunctious youth, but I would like to remind the reader that we were also *more educated*. We assumed that "more educated" must mean "more intelligent"—an assumption I am no longer willing to make. An intelligent person looks at the results of his/her actions and adjusts them to make them more productive. **An intelligent person uses objective reality as a measurement of success.** Eventually, an intelligent person can predict what will work best because he/she has carefully observed what has functioned and what has not functioned. **An intelligent person does not use his intelligence to make excuses for his failed actions or beliefs.**

We were learning from respected professors! We did not have the experience to see that the professional intellectual class, with the exception of those working in the hard sciences, was never subject to measuring its ideas against objective reality. "Publish or perish" compelled professors to come up with new ideas or new "takes" on old subjects. As long as they interested fellow intellectuals and thus contributed to achieving tenure, they were "successes". Their ideas actually functioning in the real world had nothing to do with their continuing as professors. If confronted with the failure of their ideas when applied in the wider culture, these intellectuals were adroit at pointing to every reason for the failure except for the ideas themselves (economist Thomas Sowell emphasizes this point in his *Intellectuals and Society*). As far as I can tell, the intellectuals teaching at the universities are one of only two classes of people who bear no burden when their applied ideas fail. The other is the class of skillful politicians. When politicians' policies fail, they always find a way to blame the other party. The worse case scenario is when professional intellectuals convince skillful politicians to change policies! Neither takes responsibility if the policies do not do what the intellectuals or politicians had intended. But at least, in the case of skillful politicians, an opponent can point out a politician's failures. At least aware citizens can vote out a politician! Intellectuals are not voted out either by peers or their administrations. Rather, they are given tenure (originally to protect their academic freedom), which means, except in rare cases, they can't be fired.

As good students, we absorbed the ideas of our professors and held them up as ideals whether or not they worked! Our generational momentum was so strong that, at times, it was difficult to know whether their ideas were influencing us, or our ideals were influencing them.

Despite our level of education, we were not exempt from hypocrisy. We managed to chastise, even mock the soldiers returning from Vietnam for fighting a war into which they were drafted, even though we had challenged the correctness of the draft and knew that many of them had gone to war unwillingly. We enjoyed a freer access to sex and cohabitation, but then bemoaned the increasing divorce rate, and later, the return of various social diseases. We had our excuses ready: cohabitation would actually diminish the divorce rate, and proper sex education would diminish the spread of social diseases. Maybe—but these were intellectual projections, not theories that had been tested in reality. We scorned our parents for opposing our access to drugs (when they enjoyed their liquor on weekends and had supported the repeal of prohibition in 1933), and yet we were beginning to be concerned about our friends who died during "bad trips" or who had graduated to harder drugs. We wanted social equality for those suffering under Jim Crow laws, therefore many of us marched with Reverend King and took part in peaceful protests, but after his assassination, we did not condemn the racial riots and looting—hardly Reverend King's Gandhi-inspired approach. We wanted peace and yet stayed silent when organizations that extended our beliefs in radical ways attempted to bomb police stations, the US Capitol Building, and The Pentagon. We embraced the idea that women could now prevent unwanted pregnancies via The Pill, but somehow failed to use it well enough to prevent the need for abortions. We felt women were not treated equally, but ironically, we made the measurement of a woman's equality, her assuming the masculine characteristics that she claimed to dislike. We cast aside established conventions and then wondered why society was not working better.

Too intellectual to believe we could be wrong, but not intelligent enough to measure our progress against results, we slipped into hypocritical beliefs that we would not acknowledge as hypocritical. In this way, we emulated our publish-or-perish-but-never-be-accountable professors. We saw our personal preferences as the new values that everyone should support regardless of how they played out in the real world.

By no means would I suggest that many of the things we stood for in the 1960s and 1970s were undesirable simply because they were envisioned by 19-year-olds or supported by professional intellectuals. Who would be foolish enough to argue against civil rights, women's rights, or a preference for freedom over restriction? However, any social changes will tend to destroy the traditions that organize the members of that society. No one, not even we well-educated 19-year-olds, knew how to replace the clashed icons of old conventions with satisfying and supportive new conventions.

Today, we have a society in which many people feel that every personal preference must be satisfied by either the government, or other members of society, under the threat of being labeled racist, sexist, etc., i.e. being labeled a denier of equal freedoms. Further, because feeling has become more important to many people than rationality, Freedom has been conflated with Equality, and Equality of Opportunity conflated with Equality of Outcome.

The residue of my generation's rebuke of old conventions, rather than establishing a new, functional set of conventions, has substituted a plethora of subjective preferences as if, somehow, some way, that would be sufficient to make the world free and allow people to live in peace.

Nothing can grow without some kind of change; however, when advocating change, do not simply change away from something, but also toward something. Test your changes first, if possible, or if not, be watchful and wary of how your changes are performing, and be willing to change those changes.

Conventions and customs are not unassailable, but without them there is chaos. Argue against them, if you wish, but in so doing, present an alternative that will work. If, over time, you find your alternative does not work, accept that the original convention, albeit flawed, has value. Neither NEW nor OLD is necessarily better. All things must prove their objective worth; otherwise, they are just personal preferences.

Re: CONVENTIONS

The man or nation of high culture may acknowledge to great lengths the restraints imposed by conventions and honour, but beyond a certain point, primitive will or desire cannot be curbed. — H. P. Lovecraft

...a person should first be changed by a teacher's instructions, and guided by principles of ritual. Only then can he observe the rules of courtesy and humility, obey the conventions and rules of society, and achieve order. — Xun Kuang

...anybody who follows...[a rebellious] nature...will be led into quarrels and conflicts, and go against the conventions and rules of society, and will end up a criminal. — Xun Kuang

Conventions are unstated agreements within a community to abide by a single way of doing things—not because there is any inherent advantage to the choice, but because there is an advantage to everyone making the same choice. — Steven Pinker

Traditionalism is like a pipe conducting the flow of life-giving water. Without the restriction of the pipe, the water cannot be conveyed; but, the pipe is of no use if clogged with the refuse of antiquity. — paraphrase of a Maxwell Struthers Burt quote

8.

EMOTION vs. RATIONALITY:

If an emotional message is swaying your opinion, try to understand the core belief in the message behind the emotions. Even the most forceful assertion is not the same as evidence.

Emotional messages either make you feel threatened or tug at your heartstrings because someone is suffering—sometimes both. Many of these are legitimate warnings or calls for help, in which case their core beliefs are obvious, and they use evidence rather than assertions to convince you to take action.

If you see an ad for Mothers Against Drunk Driving (MADD) with horribly contorted vehicles and teenagers who can no longer play sports because they are in wheelchairs, you not only feel bad for them, but you also take several warnings from the images: fasten your seat belt, don't drive intoxicated, and give erratic drivers a lot of road space before pulling over to call the cops. Their message is clear and the emotions they illicit serve a cause (safe driving, fewer accidents) with which you agree. Were you not familiar with the organization, you might want to check the validity of their charity before you call in a donation, but having done that, you recognize that you are not being illegitimately influenced because their emotional message comports with what you already believe and the money they receive goes where it is supposed to go.

Hospitals that ask for your donations through TV advertisements will show you images of sick and suffering children so you will feel distressed and will feel less stressed only after you call in a donation. You can't save the kids directly, you think, but you can at least help a little. If you know that a large percentage of the money you donate goes to helping those kids, the hospital's emotional appeal is honest because the message that the advertisement conveys is overt and truthful.

However, some advertisements or appeals to action stir up the emotions and draw a conclusion for you, hiding their core belief behind the overt message. Their use of emotion is to get you to act before investigating the details. The most frequent of these are political ads. When campaigns "go negative," they are trying to paint their opponents as undesirable. And their opponents are often doing the same thing. In order not to be swayed by untruths, you have to seek out the facts (see Guideline Principle #1: *Neither Tell or Believe Lies About the Other Side*), and then analyze the message.

Joseph A. Schumpeter (1883-1950) wrote, "The first thing a man will do for his ideals is lie." A very subtle way that a candidate can tell an untruth is to get you fired up about a generic principle or idea. If the idea is positive, the candidate attempts to associate himself with it. If it is negative, he attempts to associate his opponent with it.

Here is a generic principle: nuclear war is undesirable. Since that assertion is pretty difficult to deny, you might become susceptible to part two of this political tactic: associating the political opponent with nuclear war.

One of the most famous and successful political ads of all times was President Lyndon B. Johnson's ad for the 1964 presidential race in which he opposed Senator Barry Goldwater. It had been reported that Goldwater would be willing to use nuclear weapons to end the war in Vietnam. Actually, that was not precisely what he had said, but extreme positions make news so it was easier for the media to portray Goldwater as the hawk and LBJ as taking a more dovish approach.

LBJ's "Daisy Girl" ad showed a child picking petals off daisies in a field, counting them aloud. Her cute voice is overwhelmed by an adult male's voice giving a rocket countdown. The camera closes in on her face and then her right eye, which then becomes an atomic blast. LBJ then adds a voice-over: "These are the stakes: to make a world in which all children can live, or to go into the dark. We must either love each other, or we must die." An announcer then says, "Vote for President Johnson on November third. The stakes are too high to stay home."

Since this was one of the most strongly emotional appeals I have witnessed in my adult life, since it encompassed both a threat and a pull at the heartstrings at the same time, and because it is old enough not to emotionally agitate current partisans, I chose it for analysis.

In the Daisy Girl ad, no mention is made of Johnson's opponent. Also LBJ's verbal sentiment cleverly echoes both conservative Christians and the peaceniks of the sixties and seventies ("love one another"). Ironically, those peaceniks were soon to march against LBJ chanting, "Hey! Hey! LBJ! How many kids did you kill today?" But to them, in 1964, the message, although not overt, was clear: a vote for Goldwater increases the likelihood of nuclear war.

What is the origin of this core belief? It could not

have been because Goldwater's party had been the first to use nuclear weapons. It could not have been because there was an actual dichotomy between loving one another and dying. The core of the assumed belief that electing Goldwater might lead to atomic war could only exist because the press had exaggerated Goldwater's response regarding the potential of atomic weapons in Vietnam. Here's a quote from The History Channel's website:

> Senator Barry Goldwater (R-Arizona), running for the Republican Party nomination in the upcoming presidential election, gives an interview in which he discusses the use of low-yield atomic bombs in North Vietnam to defoliate forests and destroy bridges, roads, and railroad lines bringing supplies from communist China. During the storm of criticism that followed, Goldwater tried to back away from these drastic actions, claiming that he did not mean to advocate the use of atomic bombs but was "repeating a suggestion made by competent military people." Democrats painted Goldwater as a warmonger who was overly eager to use nuclear weapons in Vietnam.

So, Goldwater unwittingly provided his opposition with something it could exaggerate, and exaggerate it did, all the way to having the daisy girl (and by implication, all of us) become the victim of a nuclear war. Did the senator from Arizona really intend to use nuclear weapons to end Vietnam? Probably not. Was he a dangerous warmonger? Probably not. Would low-yield nuclear weapons, if used to defoliate some of the forests in Vietnam as some of the military were considering, lead to a nuclear war? Probably not. Nevertheless, the hidden core belief, true or not, that LBJ and company wanted to transmit was that "Goldwater equals Death".

This is not to say that Goldwater was fully prepared to deal with the hardball politics that was beginning to go to extremes in the 1960s. I think that Goldwater's chances for election were completely dashed when he stated, as most conservatives would, that he supported states' rights. He did not vote for the Civil Rights Act of 1964, where most Republicans did, because he held a principled stance regarding the constitutionality of two subsections of the bill. However, Martin Luther King stated publicly that Goldwater's stand on states' rights was *code for* the suppression of civil rights (i.e. black citizens' rights) in the southern states. Senator Goldwater was certainly not a racist. In fact he said clearly, "I am unalterably opposed to discrimination or segregation on the basis of race, color, or creed, or on any other basis...."

Goldwater's error was two fold, in my opinion: (1) he did not realize that standing on principle is often too subtle an argument to make in an age of television (and now of the Internet) in which hard simplicity and captivating images are more powerful than careful nuance (I would refer you back to the initial discussion of graphic memes in the first Guideline Principle), and (2) he did not make clear, despite his strong statement about his own anti-segregationist convictions, that although states' rights should hold sway over federal legislation, *individual rights* should hold sway over states' rights.

Dr. King unconsciously had given politicians a new weapon. His idea that one statement could be code for another is akin to our previously discussed idea of reframing, not to enhance one's personal wellbeing, but to portray the reframe as if it were objective truth. The Daisy Girl ad had made no assertions about the truth; rather, it had dealt in unspoken implications. However, Dr. King had unwittingly stated as truth something that was not true. Because he so strongly believed in the value of the Civil Rights Act of 1964, he opposed Goldwater, implying a racism that wasn't there. A celluloid child and an iconic civil rights activist had put Goldwater's presidential bid to rest.

In political contests, you are at an advantage if you can refer your audience to those labels and slurs about your opponent that have already adhered. A smear may have been proved incorrect, but people tend to remember the garish slur rather than the correction. How many times has a major newspaper published a story that was incorrect, then have to retract it? The incorrect account was headlined in bold type on the front page while the next day's retraction is tucked in a box on the bottom of page 17. In this way, an untruth can easily become a preconceived notion in the minds of the public.

Why do trial lawyers blurt out some brash accusation knowing that the judge will order it stricken from the record? It's because the jury cannot un-hear it. The accusation will leave a more lasting impression than the judge's order that it be disallowed. "The jury will ignore that last comment" is, as every lawyer knows, nearly impossible.

A label that sticks becomes a preconceived notion in your mind. And a preconceived notion that castes doubt on one side makes the job of the other side easier. However, alluding to preconceived notions makes your job   the job of trying to find the objective truth—more difficult. **People will make a statement that theoretically could be true (an hypothesis) then portray it as if it had been proven true. But, an hypothesis is not a validated conclusion.**

Companies that compete for the consumer's dollar can also use emotional ads, but usually they are not as invested in destroying the competition as they are making themselves look good. Political ads, on the other hand, are more likely to be nasty because the perpetrator of the ad is unlikely to suffer consequences—the voter will choose the candidate only once within a period of several years, and in the next election, the candidate's competitor will change, as will the relevant issues. The politician knows that there is no Consumer Reports or Better Business Bureau for candidates or their parties, therefore the voter is not likely to be well informed on either the issues or the candidates' histories. The voter forgets or ignores the nastiness of last election and focuses on the current election's conflicts. In any case, the voter not only will have a very short memory about political affairs, but also will vote on his/her impressions, rather than on the issues. The likelihood of emotional messages succeeding is therefore high.

Until someone actually creates an objective clearinghouse for political candidates and their claims (fact-checking websites are a start, but they too can be biased), individuals have to adjudicate their own reactions to emotional arguments they will face in election season (and often in between seasons, as well).

My first full year of teaching at an out-of-state private school was also a presidential election year. Before I sent in an absentee ballot, I wanted to make sure I understood the positions of the candidates. I did not have easy access to TV and the local newspaper had already taken its side, so reading its editorials would not have been informative. At the local convenience store, I discovered a magazine that for fifty cents outlined the major planks of both parties' platforms and gave a brief overview of the counterarguments to each party's positions. I scooped it up right away. I have never seen another magazine like it since that election many decades ago. Why? I suspect that one political party or another felt it was not getting a fair appraisal in the magazine. If the publication did not *favor* a specific party, *that party could claim bias*! Just the opposite of what you would expect. But the whole idea of the magazine was *not* to be like the newspapers, editorializing for their favorites, but instead to be as objective as possible. The only favorable bias in such a comparison would be toward the side that had marshaled the facts rather than the emotions. Objectivity would therefore strip one or both parties of an emotional appeal they did not want to forego.

Picture an angry protestor yelling invectives at The White House or Congress. Inevitably, he will use extreme exaggeration to cast his opposition in the most emotionally negative light possible. Witnessing this sort of thing, I use a simple guideline before setting about my research: the more extreme the invective, the less likely I think it accurate. In other words, the protestor's emotion will have aroused my emotion enough for me to jump to the conclusion that more research is needed.

In this guideline principle, I am suggesting that it is wise to recognize when something is attempting to appeal to your emotions. Valid or invalid, that appeal is an attempt to bring you to an instant conclusion without the delay and the effort of a rational review. I resist this. I also try to resist hating the person or organization that perpetrated the emotional appeal. I can issue a judgment of non-compliance and even conclude that I will not support such perpetrators and their negative tactics without needing to make them a permanent enemy. I try to follow Albert Einstein's advice: "Stay away from negative people. They have a problem for every solution."

When asked what thoughts he would leave a future generation, Bertrand Russell said, "I should like to say two things, one intellectual and one moral. The intellectual thing

I should want to say is this: When you are studying any matter, or considering any philosophy, ask yourself only what are the facts and what is the truth that the facts bear out. Never let yourself be diverted either by what you wish to believe, or by what you think would have beneficent social effects if it were believed. But look only, and solely, at what are the facts.... The moral thing I should wish to say...love is wise, hatred is foolish. In this world which is getting more closely and closely interconnected, we have to learn to tolerate each other, we have to learn to put up with the fact that some people say things that we don't like. We can only live together in that way and if we are to live together...we must learn a kind of charity and a kind of tolerance which is absolutely vital to the continuation of human life on this planet."

If an emotional message is swaying your opinion, try to understand the core belief in the message behind the emotions. Even the most forceful assertion is not the same as evidence.

9.

EMOTION vs. RATIONALITY:

Emotions help us identify our values; they do not help us determine how to appraise them, obtain them, or keep them. Only rationality can do that.

Throughout this book, I have made a case for logic, rationality, and seeking empirical evidence when it comes to making decisions because I think these methods, which used to be traditional or at least were traditionally aspired to, are now easily underplayed and overlooked. Today, because of a passive acceptance of philosophical relativism with a decided political bent, we are willing to forget about the cultural methods that produced The Enlightenment and contributed to producing The United States Constitution, many brilliant works of literature, advances in science, burgeoning economies, and civil methods by which we advance new ideas or peacefully disagree. Today, many people prefer to see logic/ rationality as just another subjective point of view—just another cultural convention that has no more value than any other. Feelings are considered of equal value to facts. Emotion is considered of equal value to reasoning in making choices, even though these functions are not for the same purpose and cannot accomplish the same ends.

Emotions are built into the older sections of the brain. They are fundamental because they exist to preserve us. Self-preservation is as *fundamental* a value as you can have. Emotions make us react with fight, flight, or freeze. When used correctly, all three primitive emotional reactions can help us survive. However, if you flee when you should fight, or fight when you should flee, or if your emotions have pumped so much adrenaline into your system that you become a deer in the headlights, those emotions won't do their job.

There is no more positive value than to be alive (and thus be able to hold other values). Thank you, amygdala and other primitive sections of the human brain! Without you and the emotions you originate, humankind would not have lived long enough to evolve the more careful and deliberate prefrontal lobe. But those same basic emotions that can protect you in one situation might harm you in another! If your fear makes you *flee* from a cheetah, it is unlikely you'll get away in time. If your anger makes you *fight* a grizzly, it is unlikely that you'll come out for the second round. If your panic makes you *freeze* at an alien predator's x-ray goggles, you will be the next victim of its ray gun.

Contemporary human beings, unlikely to face ferocious felines, ursines, or aliens, use all three fundamental reactions, but in a more calculated way. Yes, we humans want to survive, but we also know that we must *choose* the appropriate reaction to aid us, and we must figure out *how to deploy* that reaction before we run into a triple F (fight, flight, or freeze) situation. Thank you, prefrontal lobe for having gone beyond humankind's more fundamental reactions, thus giving us a fighting (or fleeing or freezing) chance to survive.

Perhaps we have faultily assessed an apparent threat. Perhaps the guy with the shotgun is not here to rob us, but to save us from the angry (read: emotional) mob marching down the street. How can we know? Emotions won't help. We have to figure out a way to get more facts, ascertain a way to evaluate those facts, and then determine a way to act on that evaluation. "Figure out", "ascertain", and "determine" all suggest a rational response.

Because cheetahs, grizzlies, or alien predators seldom threaten us, many of us do not appreciate the value of rationality in a stressful situation. Admittedly, rationality is too deliberate and slow to employ at the instant of crisis. That is why it must be employed *before* the instant of crisis. Rational effort helps determine how our emotions will be modified when the crisis occurs.

You might notice that I am suggesting rationality can inform emotion while in the Guideline Principle above I suggest that emotions help identify values. These statements may appear contradictory, but they are not. Think of it this way. Without rational evaluation, we instinctually choose life. As previously stated, that is human nature. In everyday life, even when we are not in crisis, our fundamental emotions identify what will aid our survival. Our emotions will react, for example, to a hundred dollar bill dropped by the previous customer at the grocery store. "That could buy me a quite a few groceries," they tell us. Food is important to survival, so our emotions have helped us instantly recognize that $100 is valuable to us. Note that neither cheetah nor bear (nor even alien predator) would recognize its value. However, the initial understanding that $100 can be traded for various goods must have been learned, not emoted. Remember this from the introduction? **"Knowledge is not know-how, and know-how is useless without purpose."** A person must rationally consider how best to spend the $100. Only the human skill of rationality can make the translation from a certain kind of greenish paper to how that paper can be used.

If we act on the emotion and slyly snatch up the $100 bill, thinking of neither ethics nor potential consequences, our having identified a fundamental value does not help us. The rational mind says, "This $100 bill does not belong to you. It clearly belongs to that last customer. Returning it to its owner might not result in positive consequences to you, but pocketing it might result in negative consequences to you." Even if you were not a terribly ethical person, you would still need to employ your rationality to evaluate the threat if you decided to escape with the money. Dwelling on this subject with your rational mind not only helps appraise your situation, it helps determine values your emotion will instantly identify the next time someone drops some cash, even if those values are as simplistic as deciding which is preferable, $100 or being caught with someone else's money.

Reducing that evaluation to a preconceived notion, as important as that might be, puts rationality on hold again. Since it is impractical to rationally re-evaluate every situation at every turn, it is understandable that people suspend their rationality in favor of the impressions that their rationally determined preconceived notions have provided. Every once in a while, however, it may be wise to reconsider one's preconceived notions and determine if they still pass rational muster.

It is wiser first to rationally consider problems so that our rationality has already informed our emotional evaluation when an instant reaction is called for, and later to repeat the process if only to reaffirm our rational evaluations.

What about the threat that we could lose money in an investment? That is both value-laden and potentially life threatening. Regarding investing, Ray Dalio wrote this in his book called *Principles*: "Because most people are more emotional than logical, they tend to overreact to short-term results; they give up and sell low when times are bad and buy too high when times are good. I find this just as true for relationships as it is for investments—wise people stick with sound fundamentals through the ups and downs, while flighty people react emotionally to how things feel, jumping into things when they're hot and abandoning them when they're not."

Many years ago, I got into a friendly debate with two of my adult students, both women, both slightly older than I, both well-educated, and both given toward a granola-crunchy lifestyle. One was a psychiatric nurse and the other had been a psychology and biology major in college. Perhaps I was out of my depth, but I took the position that in reaching their opinions humans do not use the left side of their brains (the logical side) as much as they use their right brains (the creative side). Of course, there was no way to prove either my position or theirs, but I learned a lot in the course of the discussion. Later, I learned that left vs. right brain was probably not the best way to take sides on this issue. I believe that I was accurate in my assessment, but to be frank, so were they. It is not only too simplistic to assign logic and rationality to the left side of the brain, but also it is inaccurate to assume the right side, allegedly the creative side, would have to be purely emotional. So, unintentionally, we were talking past each other.

Their position was something like: In every day life, people go to work and solve problems or operate machinery and therefore never have the time or inclination to appreciate the world around them or enjoy themselves, let alone create something.

My position was: People often function on automatic pilot and make decisions according to preconceived notions and instant judgments (like the "impressions" I mentioned above), and never spend time either challenging their judgments or fact-finding to improve their judgments.

Now, put both those points of view together: People work on solving their own immediate problems and are not inclined to work a little more to make a rational decision unless their job is paying them to do so.

During the right/left brain discussion, I mentioned that when I say "rationality" I do not mean simply cold, hard logic. Rather, said I, rationality is the proper use of both sides of the brain. The discussion ended there with my students thinking I had semi-capitulated. My thinking was that they were so committed to emotion that they didn't notice themselves using rational capacities to marshal arguments in defense of emotion.

Certainly, I enjoy emotional books, movies, and music as much as the next person. In fact, without emotions, what value would art offer? So emotions have to be honored as part of human nature and as signals that tell us what is important to us. Just as we value staying alive as a fundamental, we value that which makes life worth living. We get emotional when reconnecting with a loved one. We get emotional seeing a child succeed. We get emotional when the good guys finally bring the bad guys to justice. All of these things have their survival value. Emotions are undeniable indicators of value, but they are not flawless indicators. What if the reconnected love one intends to take advantage of our caring for them? What if the successful child has been a cheat? What if the good guys have been lying about the bad guys all along? In order to validate our values, we need not a knee-jerk reaction coming from deep within the oldest part of our brains, but a more mature response that is more challenging to access. We need to seek out the facts, be as objective as we can, and think clearly.

Emotions help us identify our values; they do not help us determine how to appraise them, obtain them, or keep them. Only rationality can do that.

Re: EMOTION VS. RATIONALITY

"It is by emotions that we discover…. It is by logic that we prove." — Henri Poincaré *(originally written in reverse order)*

"Emotions are not tools of cognition." — Ayn Rand

"When thoughts and instructions come to me from my subconscious, rather than acting on them immediately, I have gotten into the habit of examining them with my conscious, logical mind….

[T]he most constant struggle is between feeling and thinking….

Recognize that…the biggest threat to good decision making is harmful emotions…." — Ray Dalio

10.

BIAS:

Prejudgment and bias may be difficult to avoid completely since they are psychological shortcuts to evaluating someone or something. However, discriminating because of a bias is as irrational as assuming that individuals cannot think or act in any way, except the way their group thinks or acts. Both groupthink and the assumption of groupthink eliminate individualism. Individuals are, in the end, the smallest minority.

If we assume the desirability of rational assessment, then judging by a general impression or with an insufficient cogitation is a sort of pre-judgment. Prejudgment is cousin to "prejudice".

HAIR-ISM

There was a guy in my high school who had, for a reason that no one cared to remember, a visceral and very irate reaction every time he saw a red-headed boy from another town—not a specific redheaded boy, but *any* redheaded boy. It seemed that he would pick a fight with such a fellow if their paths should cross. His absurd, overly emotional reaction was almost fun for his comrades who kept their eyes out for redheads whenever they travelled together.

"Why is he angry at redheads?" I asked, and got answers like, "Nobody knows" or "He won't say", so I stopped asking, as did his friends. They accepted his exaggerated, dramatic response as a fact of life, important only on weekend evenings when they were cruising for trouble away from the homeport.

I suspect that he was embellishing the intensity of his alleged anger, as well as the target to which it applied (really, redheads?), simply to get his buddies' attention and to entertain them until a fight broke out. In my analytical way, I was curious at first and then it began to make me ill. In essence, the guy was practicing a sort of color bias—hairism, if you will, and his friends were enjoying the show, not caring what happened to the next ginger-topped victim they came across.

MY DAD'S NEIGHBORHOOD

My father grew up in a neighborhood populated by Italian immigrants, in which there were a few Irish families, a Jewish family, and an Arab family. Although he got along with all of them, it was not unusual for him to type them according to their families' national origins. His weren't the stereotypically negative descriptions that some people use to prejudge others; rather, they were positive descriptions, no doubt equally inaccurate when applied to an entire nationality, but at least not dismissive or cruel.

Growing up, I thought how strange it was that our country, one that praised the rugged individual from its expansionist years, could manage to characterize people by their ethnic groups. Despite this inconsistency, I could accept that categorizations of people from geographically diverse areas could be more or less accurate, e.g., Swedes would tend to be taller and blonder than Sicilians, or citizens of industrialized nations would have different skills than those of agrarian nations. Further, I could understand the advantage of "typing" a person new to your purview, before actually getting to know him, by assuming some generic characteristic. A grocery store owner, for example, might assume that Irish would likely shop for potatoes or that an Italians would likely shop for tomatoes, and stock his bins accordingly. If you were looking to open quickie lunch counter, you might reasonably assume that neither a Jew nor a Muslim would frequent a Porky Pig sandwich shop. But assumptions like these, based on a somewhat accurate but nonetheless general knowledge of a nationality (and a severely limited knowledge of the individual), can lead to greater—and less accurate—generalities. Inaccurate generalities can come dangerously close to bias. And bias, of course, leads to discrimination. But wait! That's not necessarily true! Or at least it shouldn't be.

Today, a dictionary might define prejudice as "holding ill-informed opinions", but I think that is a description of "ignorance" rather than "prejudice". Furthermore, even a presumptuously false opinion does not necessarily lead to discriminatory practices. My father might have assumed that The Irish drank whiskey *after* their evening meal while The Italians drank red wine *with* their meals, but that overgeneralization would not lead him to disliking or favoring a person in his neighborhood.

As human beings, we observe accurately that all the individuals we know have unique personalities. Further, we can collect those characteristics and observe that some of

them exist in all the members of the same family. By extension, we may even notice that a certain few characteristics
persist in the larger family clan. From these observations, we
then conclude that certain nations, to the extent that related
ethnic clans make up their population, will have national
characteristics. Recognizing characteristics accurately is
not prejudice or racism anymore than recognizing Jane has
different physical characteristics from John is sexism or that
Rhonda has red hair and Betty has brown hair is hair-ism.

We are acting in a discriminatory manner only (1)
when we assume our false judgment of a person or group
must be accurate, *and* (2) when we consequently afford or
deny that person or group privileges/rights/benefits.

"Prejudice" means "acting with prejudgment", that is
to say, we judge before we get to actually experience. But so
what? I judged my college Humanities teacher before I got
to know him, but having been proved wrong, I changed my
judgment. Had I refused to take a Humanities course because
of my false prejudgment of the teacher, I may have been
practicing a negative sort of discrimination, and *that* would
have been a bias with which one could find fault. I judged
the nature of my fifth girlfriend based on my experience with
the first four, but having been proved wrong, I changed my
judgment. Had I treated my fifth girlfriend distrustfully because the other four had previously hurt me, I may have been
acting in a discriminatory way, and *that* would have been a
bias that one could disrespect. But even those negative biases
would not per force hurt the professor or the girlfriend as
they would if they had sunk to the level of bigotry.

Estimating the characteristics of a person or group
may give you a head start in understanding them. It may also

give you a head start in judging them incorrectly. What we want to avoid, I submit, is not early judgment or even the chance of a faulty early judgment—we want to avoid acting in a way that favors or disfavors one person/group without discovering the truth about our judgment.

Our more or less synonymous terms are "prejudice", "bias", "discrimination", and "X-ism" (e.g. racism or sexism). But in my humble opinion, we are actually discriminating against those terms. To avoid X-ism, it is not the other three terms that we must avoid, but the faulty assessment of a person or group leading to actions that favor or disfavor them unjustly.

Unfortunately, this messy world has come to label so many separate groups that it is impossible to judge any person rationally and fairly without being accused of bigotry. Martin Luther King projected a time when a man would be judged not by the color of his skin but by the content of his character. Today, we seem to care less about character and more about race, gender, creed, or political affiliation. In an attempt to create a society that has no X-ism, we have given up evaluating character based on rational principles of human action, and have taken the easy way out by evaluating character based on alleged group characteristics. In order to avoid racism, we have become racist. In order to avoid sexism, we have become sexist. Et cetera.

Driving with a young woman who was working with me as a gymnastics instructor at Camp Academy, we were discussing the kids we would be teaching that summer. I mentioned that, during the school year, one of the girls was being bussed across town to a dominantly "white school". I had mentioned to her mom that it was unfortunate that she had to take such a long bus ride to and from school, thus cutting into her extracurricular and homework time. Her mom felt it was worthwhile since in her estimation her daughter was getting a better education in her new, if distant, school.

My passenger, the gymnastics teacher, concurred with the mom and then went on to cite several ways in which the government could do more to help Blacks since their test scores were consistently below test scores of Whites in our state.

"With an equal chance, they'll be fine," I said.

"No, we need to do more."

"Who is 'we'?" I asked.

"White people."

"You mean to say that black people need white people to succeed? Isn't that exactly what you want race relations not to be?"

"Oh," she said, "I never thought of it that way."

DISCRIMINATION vs. BIGOTRY

Although groups can be said to have a "character", every member of that group does not necessarily share that character. If members of the Bacciagalupe family conspire to commit a bank heist, the police do not arrest the aunts, cousins, and children of the perpetrators simply because they were Bacciagalupes. Each may have had the Bacciagalupe earlobes, but that shared characteristic has nothing to do with the personal character of the clan members. If however, 80% of the clan had criminal records, the clan's general character would probably be seen as negative. It would be understandable (albeit inaccurate) if the general public took an unfavorable view of each person with that surname.

When does a valid reputation transmute to invalid discrimination or vice versa? Not to discriminate against a liar, a thief, or a murderer is foolish, but to persist in a faulty assessment of a person or group is irrational. Bias (in the faulty assessment sense) links us back to our first general topic—Truth.

Discrimination, in its negative meaning, i.e. bigotry, is acting unfairly in regard to an individual because he or she is a member of a group. This sort of discrimination occurs because the biased party assumes that the individual object of his bias will think like his/her group, act like that group, and thus be like that group. When a majority discriminates against a minority, it is practicing groupthink because it assumes the object of its discrimination must be practicing groupthink (i.e. that all members of that group must think alike)!

Prejudice is the worst sort of faith. It allows you to believe without evidence.

Any sort of X-ism, especially when it leads to discriminatory action, is an attempt to prevent thinking. It is democracy gone awry, since it does not hold to individual rights, but implicitly supports the idea that any majority can eliminate any individual's rights based on their willing or unwilling membership in a natural or artificial group. **Mob rule may be majority rule, but that doesn't make it right.** Since only the individual can actually think, both **group-think and the assumption of groupthink are an attempt to eliminate individualism.**

Only thinking individuals can come up with ideas or organize movements. Similarly, only thinking individuals can recognize an idea as prejudiced. Whenever people decide to make an easy assessment of other people or a group by acceding to a prejudice, they are contributing to a sort of cultural bullying. The bully is usually bigger (or has a bigger group) and thinks less. He is not concerned with fact, but exerting power and preserving status. His mind is not on fairness or truth, but on getting what he wants. In other words, the bully is a kind of cheat. A cheat is a sort of liar. And a liar is a thief of truth.

It is understandable that people have biased opinions, especially if they have not had a chance to discover the truth. A personally held bias, if not acted upon, hurts no one but the holder (by his willfully insulating himself from persons of value), but as soon as a person foregoes rationality in an attempt to hurt others by acting on unverified opinions, he hurts others and makes the world messier. He is also taking the chance that, in the messy world he helped create, someone will see *him* as a member of an "inferior" minority, a minority of bigots. Someone will see *him* as an individual who does not deserve to be evaluated realistically.

Can groups even exist without being discriminatory? Shouldn't groups have a way to reasonably and legally limit their memberships? Of course! This is why there is a distinction between private limousines, for example, and public transportation. This is why there are women's clubs and men's clubs. This is why there are Portuguese-American Clubs and an Italian-American Clubs. There are Catholic churches, and Protestant churches. People have a need to gather, and they want to gather with people with whom they have something in common. People like people who are like them. In a literal sense that sort of decision is discriminatory, but is not illegal or immoral. If it were illegal or immoral to limit membership to a group, it would mean that everyone should have membership in all groups at all times. That's the same as having no groups at all.

Allowing membership based on the presence of some trait is the same as restricting a membership based on the lack of an attribute. It is and should be legal. If a black male teenager complains of racism because the Chinese Women's Septuagenarian Mahjong Club will not grant him membership, his case is absurd. The Asian women have a right to have their own little get-togethers. How many black teenage motorcycle clubs would let a 70-year-old Asian woman join? Denying membership in a private club may be discrimination in the *literal* sense, but it is not based on bigotry. And, more importantly, it is private, not public.

"Public" means "access to all", but even public facilities have rules for their use and limit their hours of accessibility. So is the public swimming pool racist or sexist if it does not allow an East Indian woman to swim at midnight? Of course not! Its restrictions apply to everyone just as its accessibility applies to everyone.

I realize these distinctions occasionally become difficult to adjudicate fairly. That's why we have the courts. But the *principle* of fair treatment is not difficult to understand.

Those people that cannot see past a short-term benefit toward a larger advantage both for others and for themselves are given to immediate solutions to their problems, or immediate ways to achieve their goals. They take the easy-way out, the unthinking, sometimes discriminatory way out. In other words, their bigoted thinking is simplistic and concrete rather than rational and principled.

Prejudgment and bias may be difficult to avoid completely since they are psychological shortcuts to evaluating someone or something. However, discriminating because of a bias is as irrational as assuming that individuals cannot think or act in any way, except the way their group thinks or acts. Both groupthink and the assumption of groupthink eliminate individualism. Individuals are, in the end, the smallest minority.

Re: BIAS

"One of the biggest problems with the world today is that we have large groups of people who will accept whatever they hear on the grapevine, just because it suits their worldview—not because it is actually true or because they have evidence to support it. The really striking thing is that it would not take much effort to establish validity in most of these cases...but people prefer reassurance to research."   — Neil deGrasse Tyson

"It's not at all hard to understand a person; it's only hard to listen without bias." — Criss Jami, *Killosophy*

"It is useless to attempt to reason a man out of a thing he was never reasoned into." — Jonathan Swift

GUIDELINE PRINCIPLES:

Points and Counterpoints

Re: TRUTH:

1.   Neither tell nor believe lies about "the other side" just because you want them to be true;

2.   Dare to be scrupulously honest even if it means losing—winning via a lie will gradually destroy you and your cause, as well;

3.   Reframe the facts to make yourself feel better, if you like, but don't represent that reframe as the objective truth.

POINT 1: I just want to be left alone to live my life. Why should I be burdened with having to research the truth about whatever political parties or news stories claim? Why should I not be able to just go about my business?

COUNTERPOINT 1: You should be allowed to do so. You do not have to research anything. But if this is your choice, you should be tolerant of what other people around you decide for your groups or for the wider culture. If you do not want to determine your own rational point of view, I would suggest not casting a vote in an election, not making a contribution, and not joining a movement.

You may not know what your values are, but if you are disappointed at having to put up with a government or a culture, in which you feel estranged, whatever you don't value will eventually appear to you. Recognizing what you do not value may encourage you to be aware of what you *do* value. How to maintain what you value, however, can be done only by conscious effort.

POINT 2: One of the greatest football coaches of all time, Vince Lombardi, is reputed to have said, "Winning isn't everything. It's the only thing!" If my opponent cheats or lies, why should I not do the same thing so that it is a level playing field?

COUNTERPOINT 2: Vince Lombardi was not known for cheating his way to victory, but for earning his titles. "Winning is the only thing" reveals his single-focused mind set, not his willingness to win at any cost.

But go ahead. Fight the opponent with his own tools. Now it's a game of who can lie more convincingly or who can cheat more deviously. You might emerge victorious, but the price you pay is that others won't trust you, and your opponents will make an even greater effort to create even more convincing lies and cheat even more deviously. This is how the world becomes "messy", and continuously less pleasant to live in.

I suggest that we refrain from treating opponents as enemies and competition as war. If we give in to that temptation, we may be able to justify our nasty tactics, but we are also creating a constant state of warfare where normal, and sometimes healthy, competition would have sufficed.

POINT 3: If I do not consider my personal reframe as my own reality, why bother reframing at all?

COUNTERPOINT 3: Truth means accepting reality the way it is, as objectively as possible, within our own narrow ability to experience the world. It does not mean intentionally narrowing that experience. Our perception of reality *has* to be subjective due to the structure of the human mind. Therefore, the human mind can fantasize all sorts of non-realities, sometimes to its own disadvantage. Living in a lovely fantasy can save us from short-term discomfort, but it does not prevent us from walking into long-term pain.

When you assume that "your own reality" is real, you prevent yourself from interacting with those who cannot share your subjectivity. Relationships become nearly impossible, and what is worse, you make choices based on "your own reality" rather than objective reality (or even the "collective illusion" of reality.) Those choices can lead you blindly off a cliff.

I never tell people how to manage their own psychology, but I do think they should hold themselves accountable for the results when they do so.

Re: COURAGE:

4. Dare to lose in love, in business, and in life—losing never lasts, but if you win all the time, you are either cheating or playing with inferior opponents;

5. "What could have been" can be painful and debilitating—realize the simple fact that it could not have been.

POINT 4: Maybe no one wins all the time, but certainly it is true that losing *does last*. You can never go back and un-lose.

COUNTERPOINT 4: Sure, the memory of the loss lasts, and memory is part of reality. In fact, Howard Bloom argues that memory is a huge percentage of an individual's concept of reality. However, if you lose the use of your car in an auto accident, you don't try to maintain the damaged vehicle as it is nor imagine that it does not have that large dent on its flank. Instead, you either repair or replace it. You can't un-lose the accident that damaged the car, as you say, but once the car is replaced, the loss of the car's utility no longer exists. You now have a repaired or replaced vehicle.

As long as a human being is alive, he/she is moving forward. I no longer live in either of the houses I grew up in, the house I was married in, the apartment I rented, the condo I owned, or any other dwelling I may have occupied. They have been passed on to someone else. My apparent "loss" wasn't a true loss because either a dwelling was sold (so I traded an asset for money), or I stopped renting (thus ceasing to trade money for an asset). Losing, winning, and trading don't last; they are in constant flux.

POINT 5: I find that thinking about what could have been helps me mentally set my ideal situation, giving me something to which to aspire.

COUNTERPOINT 5: That means you are using "what could have been" in a way that supports you, which means you are not overly pained or debilitated by it. Good for you!

Re: INDEPENDENCE:

6.   Support or contribute to any cause you can validate, not one that simply sounds good—an un-validated cause may represent the opposite of what you value. Refrain, however, from membership in movements, parties, or protests. Not only do their beliefs and means tend to change over time, but your joining may make you feel obligated to defend what they stand for, rather than think for yourself.

POINT 6: But how can I be a force for good in the world (thus making it less messy) if I don't join causes that are just? Not joining makes me less effective in changing the culture for the better or in ridding the culture of what I believe to be wrong.

COUNTERPOINT 6: Since the rebellious '60s, people have taken it upon themselves to change the world in their image. In a way, this book does the same thing in a much lower key way.

Prior to the social upheavals of the 1960s, young people (often college students), who were becoming intellectually aware but who did not like the way the world turned, opted to be depressed and retreated to their favorite Greenwich village coffeehouse to snap their fingers at bad poetry readings. It was a period like that of post-WWI's Lost Generation albeit for a truncated time. The '60s generation, of which I was a part, woke up to the idea that *not* taking action would not change a thing, and that, if we wanted something to change, we had better take the reins in our own hands. History shows many cultural and societal changes during that time, as well as protests to encourage governmental changes. As my generation matured, some members entered government in order to effect change from "the inside".

The desire to take the burden of change on ourselves was, I think, much more laudable than sitting around despondent and complaining about how society had been treating you, them, or us. So, clearly my generation took on a responsibility that few other generations had taken on. Our parents, members of The Greatest Generation, took on completely different, albeit greater responsibility, of preventing outside forces from changing the culture that they were enjoying and wanted to maintain. Ironically, my generation wanted to change many aspects of the culture that our parents wanted to preserve.

That fervor to change the world has not ebbed much in more than half a century. My personal method for improving things is to change myself and hopefully set an example for a few people along the way. I believe that real change happens philosophically first, and happens more convincingly if it is not demanded of someone else. That means lasting change happens slowly. If you prefer to attempt quicker change, you will need to join a movement. But be prepared for resistance from those who do not want quick or substantial change. Also be aware from time to time that your movement may have changed direction or tactic. Join if you like and feel good about your contribution, but then stay with it only as long as the good feeling lasts and you are proud of the successes you have achieved.

Re: CONVENTIONS:

7.   Conventions and customs are not unassailable, but without them there is chaos. Argue against them, if you wish, but in so doing, present an alternative that will work. If, over time, you find your alternative does not work, accept that the original convention, albeit flawed, has value. Neither NEW nor OLD is necessarily better. All things must prove their objective worth; otherwise, they are just personal preferences.

POINT 7: But how do I know which conventions have value and which I should try to change? Won't it take a very long time for conventions to "prove their objective worth"?

COUNTERPOINT 7: Unfortunately, yes, they often take a long time to prove their worth. Sociologists, social psychologists, and other academics can probably give you a collection of conventions that currently function successfully in certain cultures and sub-cultures, but no one can tell you if another convention would have functioned better. Attempts to change convention with political action or defiance of the convention cannot guarantee that either will work better.

If you review the list of social changes brought about by my generation, we can certainly argue that many of them were for the better, but we can also argue that some were for the worse, e.g. more equal civil rights was better for the society and the individuals concerned while more frequent use of hard drugs, in most cases, was not better for either. Those who see the unfairness of current conventions seldom can guarantee the fairness of a substitute, even if they have a substitute to offer.

I am not against social change, but I am decidedly *for* contemplating a longer-term vision than most agents of change consider. I also prefer paying attention to the direction in which a change takes us in order to evaluate if I honestly want that change to continue.

Jean-Baptiste Alphonse Karr (1808-1890), A French critic, journalist, and novelist coined a saying: *"Plus ça change, plus c'est la même chose."* ("The more things change, the more they remain the same.") I interpret this as meaning that no matter how much people try to change the circumstances of the wider world, human nature remains constant. But, I also believe the inverse: "The more things try to stay the same, the more they change." It is within human nature to try to improve things. When I wrote previously that everyone is self-interested, that did not mean that everyone was greedy for what belongs to someone else (although some are, to be sure); rather, I meant that no one would work to make himself worse off! In working to improve your own situation, you contribute to the improvement of the wider culture; so, simply by staying within your human nature, you will change things.

I prefer keeping an eye on the speedometer, the road ahead, and the GPS on a regular basis.

Re: EMOTION vs. RATIONALITY:

8. If an emotional message is swaying your opinion, try to understand the core belief in the message behind the emotions. Even the most forceful assertion is not the same as evidence;

9. Emotions help us identify our values; they do not help us determine how to appraise them, obtain them, or keep them. Only rationality can do that.

POINT 8: How does one discover a core belief without getting into the head of the person or persons who created the "emotional message"?

COUNTERPOINT 8: Admittedly, this takes some skill in analyzing emotional messages. I suggest first identifying what aspect of the message appeals to you. If, for example, the message is showing poor people in need of food, you can easily recognize that what moves you emotionally is your wanting people not to suffer needlessly.

Now comes a series of verifications ("how do I know" questions). How do I know that people are actually suffering as claimed? If there are people actually suffering, how do I know the picture truly represents the people who are suffering? How do I know that my contribution will get to the people who need it? Now, assuming that these questions are answered to your satisfaction, you might ask, "What other motivations could someone have to get me to contribute/vote/join, etc.?" Absolute certainty about someone else's core beliefs is elusive at best, but doing your best to determine why someone wants to move you emotionally will allow you to make a more informed decision, prevent your being taken advantage of, and/or will give you the confidence that you will make the right decision.

POINT 9: If my emotions help me identify my values—those things that are important to me—why should I not make judgments guided by my emotions?
COUNTERPOINT 9: You should. But, after you have rationally verified their validity.

Re: BIAS:

10.   Prejudgment and bias may be difficult to avoid completely since they are psychological shortcuts to evaluating someone or something. However, discriminating because of a bias is as irrational as assuming that individuals cannot think or act in any way, except the way their group thinks or acts. Both groupthink and the assumption of groupthink eliminate individuallsm. Individuals are, in the end, the smallest minority.

POINT 10: There seems to be a contradiction here. You say that prejudgment is normal but we shouldn't prejudge, and that acting on our judgment can be discriminatory but we shouldn't discriminate.
COUNTERPOINT 10: Because the vocabulary surrounding X-isms has subsumed almost every kind of word that could suggest a slanted opinion, exactly where one

crosses the line from preference to X-ism becomes obfuscated. People can have all the preferences they want, even if you and I do not approve of them. In their private lives, they may then make choices that we would never make. When those preferential actions ignore or remove the rights of others, those preferences fold over into an undesirable prejudice or discrimination, i.e. bigotry.

I suspect that most of us *want* to be discriminating in the broadest sense, i.e. we want to discern between seats in the orchestra and the balcony, between a driver and a putter, between a sports car and an SUV, between a Zombie that will eat your brain and a survivor of a car crash. It is acceptable to indulge our individual tastes (even if others disagree) or decisions based own our own safety. It is not acceptable to support or advocate public preferences that limit the rights or civil liberties of others. Therefore, as a personal discipline, Principle #10 suggests that you avoid even the presumption that some other group is evil, an enemy, inferior, or infectious just because they have other preferences. Refer back to Guideline Principle #1.

GUIDELINE PRINCIPLES:

A Summation

Have the courage to both tell and seek out the truth so that you will not be inaccurately biased. Your simple effort to adhere to objectivity (as best you can with the resources at your disposal) is the first step to making your way through a messy world.

Seeking out the truth when you are unsure can be technically difficult, despite your access to the Internet. It is difficult to know which sources to trust, but once you find a few trusted sources, your search becomes easier.

Memory and history is the only method by which we can evaluate what sources claim is true. Our experience is made up of what is happening right this instant, what we remember, and what is recorded. What we remember about important issues outside of our personal purview is our version of history. History has more lessons than we may care to accept.

We seem to always concentrate on what is different about our current situation as compared to the past, rather than seeing what is similar. If we can get beyond this, we can see that people in the past faced similar choices and had to confront arguments similar to those we confront in the present. We can learn from their successes and their mistakes and thus begin to trust the sources that have learned similar lessons from the past.

Although I encourage courage over cowardice, I realize that many individuals either cannot or do not wish to take bold action, so I never advocate indulging in situations that will demand extraordinary feats of heroism. My preference is "Don't deny the necessity for heroism when it occurs, but don't seek it or create the necessity, either." I believe in careful consideration, careful planning, due diligence, etc., but once preparation is sufficiently accomplished, one must act. To take no action is to go nowhere. Prepare then proceed, knowing you might win and you might not. That action is the seed for other successive actions. And those successive actions, lead one…if you will excuse the pun…to success.

Most people walk only where they can see. It is too difficult to buy a map and binoculars, or hire a trusted guide who has walked the path before. Gosh! That would mean first vetting the guide, and then prepping for the journey in the way he advises. Such a pain in the path!

To find your way in a messy world is not easy, especially if you have no guide. It is easier to let others find a way for you and then conform to the path they want to follow—even if they have not trod it before. Even if you trust an experienced guide, eventually you will have to decide for yourself if his preferred way is the best way for you. What if there is a fork in the road?

The popular easy way out is for you to ignore any predetermined paths, never even planning the excursion, but be satisfied with the short term-gain of one step at a time as if you were blind and could trust only what your walking stick touches. When you follow an idea, a cause, a group, or a leader blindly, it is not because you cannot see, but because you will not see. When you will not see, focusing is no longer a burden—you will need to take only one cautious step at a time. But what if the leader or everyone else in the group starts running? Most people take the one-step-at-a-time route, not out of simple caution, but out of intentional blindness. When it comes time for a decision, they depend not on the map, not even on a trusted guide, but on either vague appearances or their internal impressions of their comrades running ahead of them.

Some people dislike current conventions so they go about fighting battles against conventions the destruction of which they hope will "set them free". But they are often fighting battles that have been determined by others. The apparent nobility of their chosen cause blinds them to the unspoken objectives of the cause and especially its unintended consequences.

In today's messy world, in an effort to avoid "X-isms" (racism, sexism, homophobia, etc.), people not only join groups, but also find groups to oppose. Some people feel that they cannot be set free unless they oppose some collection of evildoers allegedly preventing their freedom. If you join groups that stand *against* other groups rather than work for something, what will you do once you succeed? Seldom do groups dissolve themselves declaring success, rather they find a new mission; in this case, they find some other group to stand against. I would prefer to stand *for* something without actively trying to destroy those who disagree. Sure, I want my positions to emerge victorious, but if the other side fails, I want it to fail because it loses adherents since that side's position has lost credibility, not because my side has tried to sabotage it.

Because emotions are more fundamental and respond more quickly than the later developed rational part of the mind, people appeal to them to win arguments or to sway support their way. A moment's reflection will tell you that all emotional "arguments" are either very rudimentary arguments or not arguments at all. (NB: here, *argument* means a case, a reason, a contention, or a claim.) And yet they are disproportionately successful because Madison Avenue and Hollywood have become experts at employing emotional appeals and the rest of us have learned from the experts.

You seldom see a direct emotional appeal like this: an image of a poor, dirty crying child with a voiceover saying, "Contribute to Senator Schulz. He'll help." We are far too sophisticated to be swayed by such a crude attempt to manipulate our emotions. However, if we show a picture of Schultz's opponent sneering and the voiceover adds, "Vote against the policies that will take away the generous gifts of life from our country. Vote for Senator Schulz's Gulf Relief Campaign," we are much more likely to respond positively to Senator Schultz. Research and investigation (and perhaps listening to the other side) might change our emotional mind. They might reveal that Schultz plans to raise the gas tax to fund the "generous gifts of life". We might also find that the images used were from a Typhoon zone in Indonesia, relief for which Schultz did not support, and that the Gulf relief effort is drawing to a close and was already fully funded, anyway.

Remember the saying, "If you don't stand for something, you'll fall for anything"? I suggest standing for facts before falling for emotional appeals.

I do not believe that by personally adhering to ten guideline principles, we can solve all the problems that the modern world sends our way. But I do believe that whether we contribute to solutions or not, we have to first take care of our own character. You may not be able to find solutions to cultural challenges, but people of good character do find those solutions eventually. Perhaps it is more accurate to say that people of good character find methods of *improvement.* So often we use the word "problem" when we are demanding a "solution" from the government or other people. We have come to think that there is a solution to every problem so calling something a problem simply means activating a solution. Unfortunately, many "solutions" create new problems. I would suggest seeking improvements, instead, starting with one's own behavior.

Maintaining that good character and rational thinking is a sort of proactive "broken windows" policy. The Broken Windows theory was introduced in a 1982 article by social scientists James Q. Wilson and George L. Kelling. Picture a building with several windows facing a lot. The lower pane of one window has been broken. In a short time, some mischievous someone will break another pane, and then panes in another window. The concept is that if the first pane remains unrepaired, clearly no one cares about the other panes. That gives the mischievous among us "permission" to do more damage. Soon other windows, then the building, and then the neighborhood, is trashed. Conversely, if little repairs are made, it is obvious that the building remains cared for, and fewer mischievous breaks will occur.

My way of looking at the messy world is (1) I can't fix much of anything directly, but (2) I can fix me. I can do my best job at being my best me. If I do not allow my windowpane to be broken in the first place, I contribute to making the world a less messy place.

RE: PRINCIPLES

"While good principles and policies almost always provide good guidance, remember that there are exceptions to every rule.... Exceptions should be extremely rare because policies that have frequent exceptions are ineffective."　—Ray Dalio

APPENDIX

The 8 Rules
George Washington Carver
lived by:

1. Be clean both inside and out

2. Neither look up to the rich nor down to the poor

3. Lose, if need be, without squealing

4. Win without bragging

5. Always be considerate of women, children and older people

6. Be too brave to lie

7. Be too generous to cheat

8. Take your share of the world & let others take theirs

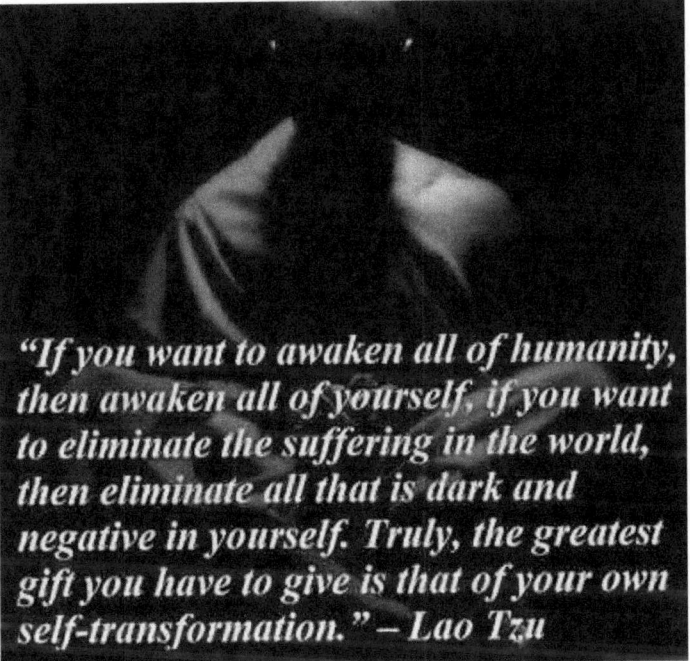

"If you want to awaken all of humanity, then awaken all of yourself; if you want to eliminate the suffering in the world, then eliminate all that is dark and negative in yourself. Truly, the greatest gift you have to give is that of your own self-transformation." – Lao Tzu

This quote is from the Hua Hu Jing, not regarded by scholars as by Laozi ("Lao Tzu" is the older Wade-Giles Romanization).

"You will continue to suffer if you have an emotional reaction to everything that is said to you. True power is sitting back and observing everything with logic. If words control you that means everyone else can control you. Breathe and allow things to pass."
- Bruce Lee

BIBLIOGRAPHY

Bloom, Howard, Global Brain, John Wiley & Sons, Inc., 2000.

Robbins, Mel, The Five Second Rule, Simon & Schuster, 2017.

Robbins, Tony, Unlimited Power (audiocassettes), Nightingale-
Conant, 1986.

Ruiz, Don Miguel, The Four Agreements, Amber-Allen Publishing,
Inc., 1997

Sowell, Thomas, Intellectuals and Society (CD program), Black-
stone Audio, 2010

White, Jamie, Crimes Against Logic, McGraw-Hill, 2004

Wilson, Edward O., Consilience: The Unity of Knowledge, Vin-
tage Books, 1999

ABOUT THE AUTHOR

Tony Annesi's writing started with poetry and short fiction (the first stories of 1969: Loss of Innocence were drafted in 1969) and then followed his martial arts career with columns for INSIDE KARATE MAGAZINE (*Tales of the Dojo* and *The Dojo Files*) and articles for MARTIAL ARTS MASTERS, SELF-DEFENSE WORLD, INSIDE KUNG-FU, THE INTERNATIONAL FIGHTER, and BLACK BELT. He has authored *Cracking the Kata Code, The Road to Mastery, Principles of Advanced Budo, Sudden Attack Defense, Elevated Elementals, Comparative Aiki in Action,* and several volumes of essays called *Sunday with Sensei's Journal.*

In 2015, after 12 years of work, Tony completed a fantasy novel trilogy entitled *The Shangrilla Artifacts*. In 2018, he published the sequel, *An Atlantis of One.*

www.ingramcontent.com/pod-product-compliance
Lightning Source LLC
Chambersburg PA
CBHW072047280526
45788CB00006B/2212